DOWN

TO

EARTH

Edited by AMY THAXTON
Photographs and Design by ANTHONY THAXTON

Printed in the United States of America

Published by BREADBOX RESOURCES
A division of STONE SOUP

For more information, visit www.breadbox.tv
E-Mail Steve: brosteve13@gmail.com

Write to us:
BREADBOX RESOURCES
1611 Williamswood Drive Raymond, Mississippi 39154

DOWN

TO

EARTH

A 40 DAY LENTEN DEVOTIONAL

STEVE CASTEEL

Host of *The United Methodist Hour*

FOR CINDY
My beautiful wife

You have always grounded me in love
and kept me *Down to Earth*

ACKNOWLEDGEMENTS

Special thanks to Anthony Thaxton - great friend, encourager, and creative genius; Amy Thaxton for pulling it all together; *The United Methodist Hour* for giving me the privilege of sharing the Gospel on television and Clinton First United Methodist Church for allowing me to be a part of an awesome family of God.

INTRODUCTION

"In the beginning was the Word and the Word was
with God and the Word was God . . .
The Word became flesh and made His home among us"
John 1:1,14
Common English Bible

THE CREATION STORY is a love story, God and the earth. The love is so deep that the creator of all things made this incredible universal garden and then took a little dirt and made us, blew life into us. It was *good!*

Then that living earth broke God's heart. God's response was to come *down to earth.* God searched for Adam and Eve in the Garden. God hung a rainbow in the sky for Noah. God came to Moses in the burning bush and led the Israelites through the wilderness. The Word is always making a way to be among us. This isn't some idealist theology. It is practical truth. Isn't that the meaning of *down to earth?* God has always been a *down to earth* God.

Jesus is the ultimate example of this. He came *down to earth* in the most humble of settings. He was a little boy and grew up in a very *down to earth* life. Then Jesus took to the wilderness to prepare for his ministry. Forty days of living in the heart of the earth. Jesus called down to earth disciples like fishermen and tax collectors. He ate and hung out with the "earthiest" kind of people. Some were prostitutes and scoundrels. Some folks thought he got his hands too dirty.

His teachings were *down to earth* parables. He talked about lost coins, lamps, weddings, and harvest.

His parables were practical stories of real life. He taught on hillsides and did miracles with mud. His followers were the poor and lepers. His life was taken when he was beaten to a bloody pulp and crucified like some common criminal. He was placed in the very earth he made. And then . . . He came *back* to earth.

Lent is a journey *back* to earth. It is our call to dig in our "dirt" and allow God to birth us again. I hope that as you read these devotionals it will be a grounding experience (pun intended). These 40 days are designed to help you fall more deeply in love with the God who made you and who wants you to have life here and into forever.

> *"For God so loved the world that*
> *He sent His Son down to earth!"*
> (Casteel translation)

DAY 1: SUNDAY

READ SCRIPTURE: HEBREWS 13:12

During Lent, many commit to fasting or giving up certain types of luxuries as a form of penitence. As we begin this season of bringing Christ *down to earth* in the Easter story, I thought of a recent example of a father's sacrifice.

My friend Anthony is a history lover. Having the chance to fly in the famous B-17 bomber, *Memphis Belle*, Anthony, instead, allowed his son to take the flight. Anthony reflected, "Bryant had never flown anywhere. What an experience it would be for a child to say his first flight was in a World War II B17 bomber!"

I know that it required a real sacrifice on Anthony's part. He would've loved to have flown in that historic aircraft. Anthony is crazy about history. But more than that, he is crazy about his son.

As a father, Anthony made a sacrifice so that his son could experience something special. It makes me think about the sacrifice of God because we are all His children. He wants us to experience life abundant, to experience kingdom life together.

And by doing that, God had to sacrifice. He had to move heaven and earth to be able to allow us to be with Him. Jesus had to come down to us, come down to earth. What great love that was!

YOUR STORY

The Lenten season is our most vivid reminder of God's sacrifice. Like the preceding example of a father giving up his place for his son, what are examples that you can think of in your own past where sacrifice for love is evident?

_____

_____

_____

What is something you can give up for the next forty days to serve as a constant reminder to yourself of God's sacrifice in sending Jesus to our needy world?

_____

_____

_____

_____

PRAYER PROMPT

Ask God for strength to sacrifice the time and energy it will take to complete this devotional guide. Pray for Him to speak to you through this journey.

DAY 2: MONDAY

READ SCRIPTURE: ROMANS 12:1,2

It's time for us to get real about our journey. If we are to see Christ as He truly was, we might have to sacrifice how we view ourselves. We have to honestly be able to evaluate where we are on our journey to the cross. We can't truly be the people God wants us to be unless we are aware of our location.

I know too many people caught up in trying to please other people. They are so caught up in trying to be what they think other people want them to be that they miss themselves.

Jesus gave two great commandments. First He said, "Love God." His second commandment is to "love your neighbor as you love yourself."

Part of the truth of your love being able to bloom is being able to live into loving yourself. God wants you to trust who you are in Him, to know that He is enough. He wants you to claim that no matter what age you are, no matter what your gift set is... you are to trust that you are one of God's gifts to the world. You are a gift to somebody.

Whether you're just that worrisome neighbor who calls and checks on somebody after seeing a stranger around their house, or whether you're that person who writes that thank you letter to everybody. You might be like my mother-in-law. She always made sure everybody got a birthday card. She knew you and you couldn't wait to get the card. That was one of her gifts to each of us.

Now, what do you have to give?

It's only by giving ourselves away and really claiming our unique gifts and talents and tastes and desires that we live into the kingdom promise of God.

YOUR STORY

God made you *you*! What are small ways in which you affect those around you with thoughtfulness?

_____

_____

_____

Learning to love ourselves and feel confident that we belong to our Father is an important part of being able to trust enough to love others. What are the things in your life that are keeping you from loving yourself? What can you do about those things?

_____

_____

_____

_____

PRAYER PROMPT

Ask God for strength to sacrifice the time and energy it will take to complete this devotional guide. Pray for Him to speak to you through this journey.

DAY 3: TUESDAY

READ SCRIPTURE: JAMES 1:2-4

Real life sometimes hurts. It's that simple.

As we begin our journey towards Easter together, there's no use denying the hard parts of life. In fact, that's the whole point of this study. We want to be *down to earth* as we realize exactly what that means for our lives.

So there are hard parts. Death, worry, stress, pain. These are things with which we are all too familiar. And there's something that's always intrigued me with the way we handle these situations in our own lives and in the lives of those around us.

In the faith, the scripture tells us again and again and again that tribulation and trial, through perseverance, shapes us into better people.

You know what? Sometimes, I don't believe that. The truth is I'm a very impatient person. I want what I want when I want it and I want things fixed now. I want to be able to say I have a problem, then it's gone. Poof. Magic. Instant. Microwave.

But, scripture tells us again and again and again that life is formational, that's it's more like growing an oak than microwaving a biscuit. And that's hard for us to wrap our minds around.

And all that suffering and tribulation? Well, problems cannot be good, can they? Well, the scripture says yes. Many times, it's those things that truly prove and test and shape our character and make us into the people we are. Or it makes us into the people we wish we were. James says, "Consider it pure joy, my brothers, when you face trials of many kinds because you know that the testing of your faith develops perseverance, perseverance must finish His work so that you may be mature and complete, not lacking anything."

This litany of perseverance and formation may be hard to accept, but God's word says that it's true.

YOUR STORY

Have there been trials in your life where God seemed far away? Describe that feeling.

_____

_____

_____

_____

What thoughts of comfort can you find in the passage above from James?

_____

_____

_____

_____

When you see others suffering and going through tests of faith, what are specific, down to earth ways in which you can help through actions and not words?

_____

_____

_____

_____

_____

PRAYER PROMPT

Ask for God's help in the trials you currently face. Then spend more time asking for God's intervention in the trials of those you love.

DAY 4: WEDNESDAY

READ SCRIPTURE: LUKE 11:5-12

Moving forward doesn't just mean being able to sacrifice or being able to persist in difficult times. It also means taking care of ourselves, maintaining the temples God has given us. We need to talk about being healthy in our lives as well as in our faith.

When talking of physical health, I think about Luke's Gospel. Luke was an ancient day physician and was very concerned about wellness. He told about many healing miracles within his gospel. That was the way he looked at the life of Jesus.

The current reality, however, is that our churches don't do healing services much anymore. In this modern day, this technological world, that kind of conversation scares us. But Jesus constantly reminded us to ask for what we want. God doesn't skirt around that, even when it comes to healing. Luke, chapter 11, tells us:

> Don't bargain with God. Be direct. Ask for what you need.
> This is not a cat-and-mouse, hide-and-seek game we're in. If
> your little boy asks for a serving of fish, do you scare him with
> a live snake on his plate? If your little girl asks for an egg, do
> you trick her with a spider? As bad as you are, you wouldn't
> think of such a thing—you're at least decent to your own
> children. And don't you think the Father who conceived you
> in love will give the Holy Spirit when you ask him for it?

I love that passage. One of the things I discovered after quadruple bypass surgery was that many times, when I was feeling broken and inadequate, I was scared to ask God. Honestly, I asked myself *What if He doesn't heal me? What if it doesn't happen? Does that mean I'm not faithful enough? Does that mean that I've made a mistake? Does that mean that I don't know how to ask?*

Well scripture says we have a God who wants us to go straight up to Him. If our body is broken, we say "God, I need some help." If our heart is broken, we say "God, I need some help." If our mind or our spirit or any part of us is broken and needs healing, we just ask for that help.

Recovering from surgery, I prayed a lot. God did not accelerate the healing of my body, which just takes time. But what He did was to send angel after angel, person after person, to sit with me as I healed.

And you know what? In a powerful way, that was healing. It brought me a sense of renewal, a sense of not being alone. It brought a sense of wholeness.

YOUR STORY

When were the times in your life in which you needed healing? Did you ask for help? Did you recognize the help God sent?

_____

_____

_____

_____

_____

Have you read the Gospel of Luke lately? Miracles still happen today, but why not read Luke's accounts to find inspiration before moving forward on our journey towards Easter? After reading some of these stories, journal your reactions below:

_____

_____

_____

_____

_____

PRAYER PROMPT

Pray for healing for your mind and body. Be specific. Pray for the healing of others, both physical and of spirit.

DAY 5: THURSDAY

READ SCRIPTURE: ACTS 2:42-47

I know a lot of you have been burned by the church. I've heard quite a few people say, "The church is full of sinners."

Guess what? They're absolutely right. That's why we're there, trying to be healed and made whole in the power of Jesus Christ!

I hope you take time today and you begin to pray about God healing your heart and your soul where the church and its people are concerned.

Church has done things that are unspeakable to many. Some of you have just become disillusioned and disappointed. Some have just drifted away from God and think a little 30 minute snippet might just be your fix that makes you feel good long enough to think you've done a God thing.

Let me tell you that's not enough. You need to be a part of a congregation. You need to be surrounded by other believers. We were not made to live alone in faith. In Genesis, the only place in the creation story that God said "It is *not* good" is when He created Adam and says it is not good that Adam should be alone.

It's not good that you be alone in your faith walk. We need you to be a part of the body of Christ; to literally bring yourself to the body as a donation to its life and health. No body of Christ is complete without every body. We are the cellular structure of the kingdom. Each of us, hand, foot, head, eyes, ears, mouth, and other parts all need to be a part of the body if the kingdom is genuinely to come.

There's a congregation waiting for you to be a part. The church doesn't need you just to attend occasionally. The church needs for you to *be the church*. If church is broken, help fix it.

YOUR STORY

Do you attend church? If so, what are the ways you're involved?

_____

_____

Okay, in what ways do you hold back? What do you keep for yourself rather than sharing for the kingdom work? Are there things you can do to "let go and let God?"

_____

_____

_____

There are those who are homebound or in nursing homes who need to be a part of a congregation as well. Plan time in the near future where you can care for those in need of companionship.

PRAYER PROMPT

Pray for God to lead you in the right paths where church is concerned. Pray for Godly friends to accompany you as you go. Pray for the broken areas and ask His touch and healing. Ask God to clearly show you places where you should serve.

DAY 6: FRIDAY

READ SCRIPTURE: JOHN 15:13,14

One of the people that has grown near and dear to me is Suzanne Walters. After surviving through a series of autoimmune disorders, Suzanne had tragedy after tragedy in her life. At this time, she is still wrestling with a liver that is failing.

Suzanne is a huge proponent of organ donation. Again and again Jesus said, "Greater love has no person than they lay down a life for a friend." To be an organ donor is to take that seriously, literally. It says that I'm willing to take what I can no longer use once I'm freed from this body and give it as a gift to somebody who may need a part of me.

I've always had good intentions about being a donor, but it took Suzanne's friendship to help convince me to follow through and become the official organ donor that I have now signed up to become. Suzanne's example is extra special to me, because her story and my story have become connected.

It happened like this. Suzanne's health kept her from attending church, and she became a viewer of my television program, *The United Methodist Hour*. While watching my message one week, Suzanne was moved by my invitation to not be "lukewarm." My urging viewers to do something *where they were* encouraged Suzanne to find ways to serve others even in her situation.

Out of this, Suzanne created this incredible blog called *Places of Hope*. It is this litany of people with story after story after story. It's a support page for people who are waiting on organ transplants and people who have been through organ transplants. Her site has become one of the largest supportive blogs regarding organ donation on the web.

When we think we can do nothing, God has work for us. When we think we are useless, God has something in store. And it might just be that we can find our true call in those times of desperation.

YOUR STORY

There are very few times when we literally can give the gift of life. What would keep you from becoming an organ donor? Are you willing to consider signing up on the back of your Driver's License?

_____

_____

What limitations in your life are keeping you from being involved in some group?

_____

_____

_____

Look around and think of ways that are possible for you to still make a difference even from where you are located. List at least five ways you can serve others below:

_____

_____

_____

_____

_____

_____

_____

PRAYER PROMPT

Pray for Suzanne Walters and others like her on the Organ Waiting Lists. Pray for their families and for strength. Ask God to show you ways you can make a difference in the lives of others.

DAY 7: SATURDAY

READ SCRIPTURE: JAMES 1:4-8

I live a lot of my life in my head, and that's kind of a scary thing.
We all have this gift of a mind, and a lot of Jesus' teaching centered
around what we think about, what we focus on, what we pay
attention to.

I know in my own life I find myself walking around in the
corridors of my brain, opening doors, walking around in hallways
that I probably have no business walking around in, thinking about
things that take on a life of their own. Do you understand what
I'm saying? Have you ever just created a reality in your head that
really wasn't a reality, had an argument with somebody when they
weren't even present? Ever gotten yourself into a frenzy and raised
your blood pressure about something you imagined could happen
but never really did?

Our mind is a powerful thing. Our imagination has the capacity to
create worlds.

One of the things that fascinated me on the computer was the SIM
games. These simulation games allowed you to build a city or
company. One could create avatars, letting you take on a role in a
life within that virtual reality.

Our brain has the capacity to undo what's real. It can create that
kind of simulated world through worry and our imagination. And
sometimes, that takes its toll in the worst of ways.

The book of James says, "If you don't know what you're doing, pray
to the Father. He loves to help. You'll get His help and won't be
condescended to when you ask for it. Ask boldly, believing without

a second thought. People who worry their prayers are like wind-whipped waves. Don't think you're going to get anything from the Master that way, adrift at sea, keeping all your options open."

Isn't that incredible? Don't take a second thought, pray to God when you give Him time. Don't worry your prayers.

YOUR STORY

What type of things do you imagine even though they're not real?

_____

_____

List three areas you'd like to give over to God's control through prayer:

_____

_____

_____

PRAYER PROMPT

Worrying your prayers rather than boldly asking keeps us from experiencing all God has to offer us. Ask God's help on the items listed above. Ask boldly and believe. Freely pray without worry and thank God for His goodness.

DAY  8: SUNDAY

READ SCRIPTURE: ACTS 2:16-18

Black History Month is celebrated every February. It reminds us that there was a time in our culture and in our country when there was this imaginary separation of people.

It was this perception of how people were that we carried around, that because somebody's skin was different from us, because somebody's livelihood was different from us, because somebody lived in a different part of town and had, in our culture, been separated for one reason or another, there was this other reality that maybe they thought differently, felt differently, or acted differently.

Our minds can lead us to places where we create that reality and live into it, even though it's not true.

Black history month is an incredible reminder that across racial and cultural lines, there is a humanity that is filled with emotion, relationship, and basic, fundamental things that are a part of everyone's lives. When we push our imaginations aside and we allow ourselves to be really present with each other, we find the incredible gift we have from each other.

What kind of reality do you live in? What kind of dream? Dream is also a part of imagination in our minds. For Martin Luther King, the dream was a glimpse of a reality God had given him, of a way things really should be.

That's the dream we seek to live into every week. As we continue to learn our way in how to live together, my prayer for you is that you're actively seeking out ways to live into this dream where regardless of race, color or creed, we all find ourselves living as children of God, in a kingdom that was designed to live loved.

So, ponder on those things, think on those things, and allow them to shape and form you.

YOUR STORY

Do you strive to see the person within rather than seeing race, income or status? If so, when are times that this is difficult?

_____

_____

_____

_____

The Gospel is for everyone. God loves His children. List two people with whom you need to seek a better relationship of understanding.

_____

_____

PRAYER PROMPT

Thank God for His not being a respector of persons. Ask for help in overcoming the stereotypes, prejudices, judgments and evaluations that keep us from loving like Jesus. Seek forgiveness for when you've failed, but thank God for those times He's led you to do right things.

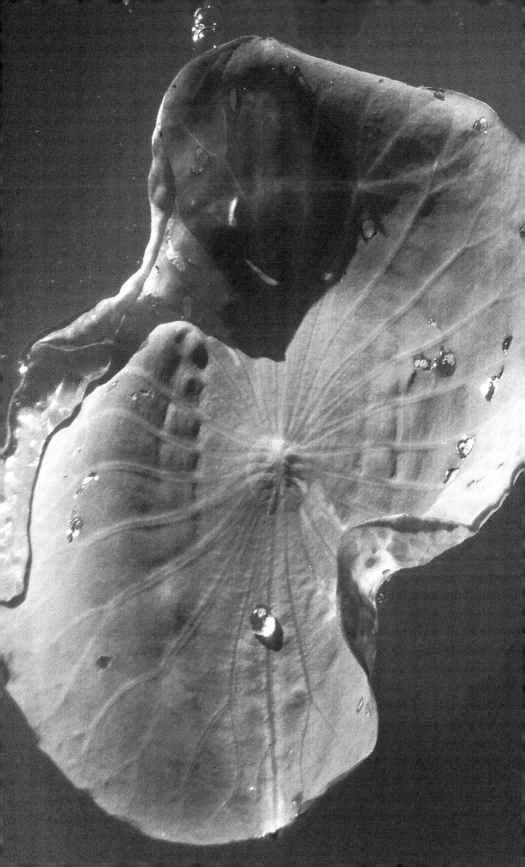

DAY 9: MONDAY

READ SCRIPTURE: MATTHEW 6:25-34

James talked about the whole issue of prayer. He said as you talk to God, as you live your life, there's a thought process that goes on.

One of the things he admonishes us about is not worrying our prayers. I have to confess that sometimes I'm like that little three year old in the line at Wal-Mart by the candy stand. "Momma, can I have this? Momma, can I have this? Momma, can I have this?" I keep asking until I think I'm going to wear God down in my prayers. I ask, I worry, I think, *Is God going to answer, is God going to do?*

One of the things James says later is that it is in perseverance and patience and waiting and faith in God that our character is shaped and that we find ourselves building confidence in God. Once we've handed something to God, we let God have it.

As I think about worry in my life, nine times out of ten, that worry is centered around my inability to let things go, my inability to trust that I have a God who is ahead of me and before me and that whether I even pray or not, that God is intent on giving me a life that is the best life I can have.

Sometimes, as people of faith, we find ourselves thinking that by the sheer emotional energy of thinking about something, of worrying about something, of walking around in something, that we can change things.

Now, I don't know if any of you have ever had an encounter with a skunk. I had a friend who had a skunk that sprayed him. When he went home, my friend tried to wash off. He tried to clean, but you could smell him from a country mile. His mother ended up giving him a tomato juice bath that eventually kind of took some of the odor. But the deal was that once that scent had gotten on him, it stuck on him and he couldn't get it off without time and patience.

Worry is like that. When we walk around in worry, it sticks to us. And that worry begins to collect and develop into a kind of cynicism. It develops and begins to smell like doubt. It clings to us and begins to cut a stream through our mind that erodes confidence, that erodes relationships. Do you know what I'm talking about?

Have you ever just walked around in something so long, stayed in your head with it, that you have come back out into conversations and life and you're angry and you don't know why? You're depressed and you don't know why? It's because sometimes we get locked up here, and we worry our way through life.

Jesus said, "What good is worry? Will it help you grow? Will it change a thing?" It's only an imaginary encounter.

YOUR STORY

What is it that you worry about? What is it that concerns your thoughts?

_____

_____

_____

_____

List those things that take your emotional energy and somehow weaken your spirit by their presence.

_____

_____

_____

_____

_____

_____

PRAYER PROMPT

Pray to be relaxed and centered. Ask to be focused, and attentive, not worrying through life, not finding yourself trying to micromanage God's universe. Specifically lift up the listed items above and hand those over to God.

DAY 10: TUESDAY

READ SCRIPTURE: JOHN 14:23

I had a memorable conversation with Wayne Muller, who is my spiritual advisor. Wayne threw out a very powerful image to me.

He presented the idea of where we make our home. He was talking about many of us making our home at work rather than making our home at *home*.

Sometimes I find myself making my home in my mind. I live in this Steve-simulated world. My imagination and my thoughts form and shape reality even though my actual reality is very different. I encounter a lot of people whose thought world destroys their real world, whose worry slowly bleaches their energy away, their love away, their life away.

So how do you deal with it? It's very simple. James says pray and trust God. Wait for God to do a God thing. God is always on time.

And if we could truly believe that, then we find ourselves praying a different kind of prayer.

YOUR STORY

Where do you make your home, at work or at home? And if we were to ask others close to you the same question about you, would their answer be the same?

_____

_____

_____

_____

What changes need to be made in your everyday life to wait on God
to do His thing?

_____

_____

_____

_____

PRAYER PROMPT

Pray with someone else today. Gather a spouse or a parent or
child... pray together for God to help make home a priority for you.
If no one is available, pray for those who made you feel at home
and seek guidance in giving that security to others.

DAY 11: WEDNESDAY

READ SCRIPTURE: MATTHEW 6: 9-13

We've talked several days about worry and prayer. Lately, I've found myself praying one simple prayer again and again and again. It's the excerpt from the Lord's Prayer. It is my reminder that I'm not in control of the world, that my imagination, my worry can never change the world.

That prayer is simply this: *Thy kingdom come, Thy will be done.* This is a reminder that no matter what I think about, I don't have the capacity to recreate this world. My best expression and use of my brain and my energy is encountering the reality in front of me in faith and trust in God.

When I can do that, I find myself breathing easier. When I can do that, I see my facial expressions ease. When I can do that, people around me notice that the edge of anger or stress is gone from my voice. The frenzy is gone from my pace.

Jesus had this way of sensing when he was being captured by his thoughts and worry. He would always go aside and talk with God. He didn't try to convince God to fix what was wrong. He found that just having that conversation brought peace because He believed God always had His best interest at heart.

That's the kind of God we serve. That's the kind of life to which we're called, the kind of incredible gift we're given. It's not a gift where we live inside our head and our virtual reality, but a gift in which we live into the will and grace of God. It's not mindlessly going about our life, but it's thinking on the right things.

What is it Philippians 4 says? *Whatever is good, whatever is pure, whatever is just, whatever is right, whatever is beautiful, whatever is virtuous, think on these things.* And then your life looks really different.

YOUR STORY

What does it feel like when you allow Him to be God and you simply let go?

_____

_____

_____

What keeps you from praying, "Thy kingdom come, Thy will be done"?

_____

_____

_____

_____

PRAYER PROMPT

Thank God for His patience. Thank God for your imagination, and pray that you learn how to use it well.

DAY 12: THURSDAY

READ SCRIPTURE: JAMES 1:19-25

Over the next few days of our journey together, we're going to talk about what it means to have personal holiness and social holiness; how do you take care of your soul and serve the kingdom of God at the same time without losing one or the other?

It's one of the big dilemmas of Christianity: how do we take care of our relationship with Christ and, at the same time, take care of our relationship with other people. Taking care of our soul and taking care of the world.

Many times, in this world of faith, people are lined up as either liberal or conservative. The liberals are out saving the world; the conservatives are saving their souls.

The truth is that Jesus meant for us to do both. There's no breaking life in half like that.

One of the tasks of learning how to live in faith is learning how to find the balance between building and cultivating intimacy with God and living into a way of acting on that faith in a way that changes the world through service and relationship.

So in the next few days, I hope you will begin to look at your own life and ask yourself, "Which end of the spectrum do I fall on? And how can I find ways to strengthen the part of myself that needs strengthening?"

PRAYER PROMPT

Ask God to speak to you in a real way through these daily times.

Day 13: Friday

I have a friend who owns many antiques. One of my favorites is an old Victrola. The cool thing about this Victrola is that it's really two machines in one. One is a mechanism that turns and spins the record as it plays. The other is the mechanism that's designed to pick up the sound and project the sound in a way that is audible.

Faith is a lot like that. It has two components. There is the inside component that gets us going. It is, as Jesus said, the first two parts of the Great Commandments. *Love God with all your heart and mind, soul and strength, and love yourself.*

Personal holiness is about the work we have in our relationship with God; getting to know God, getting to hear God, getting to put ourselves in a position where we are in intimate relationship with God.

Tony Campolo talks about the dynamics of spiritual formation and the practices that allow us to get to know God better. He teaches prayer life, scripture life, and those things that allow us to come to know God by immersing ourselves in the Word of God and the presence of God.

Now the other side of that is the God of action. Tony Campolo has long been a social activist. He's been somebody who's been about the work of working with the poor, of dealing with the disenfranchised, of living life in the fringes. Many times, because of his conservative background, some of his colleagues critiqued him as being too liberal and not paying enough attention to theology and scripture.

I've heard those conversations before. What I really believe is what James writes. We are to pay attention to both aspects.

We are to seek social holiness and personal holiness.

YOUR STORY

Which side do you practice more easily, social or personal holiness? Explain:

_____

_____

_____

What are some ways you can strive to be better balanced in this pursuit of balance?

_____

_____

_____

_____

PRAYER PROMPT

Pray for teachers like Tony Campolo who fuel our discussions. Ask God to show you areas of improvement and ways to try to please Him with all your actions.

DAY 14: SATURDAY

READ SCRIPTURE: JAMES 2: 8-12

What good is it, my brother, if a man claims to have faith but has no deeds? Can such a faith save him? Suppose a brother or a sister is without clothes or daily food, if one says to him I wish you well, keep warm and well fed, then does nothing for his physical needs. What good is it?

In the same way, faith by itself is no good if it doesn't accomplish action out of the love of Christ. Some will say we have faith. I have deeds. Show me your faith without deeds and I will show you your faith by what I do.

You believe that there is one God. Good. Even the demons believe that and shudder. God wants evidence, faith without deeds is useless.

Eugene Peterson's translation is graphic. It says separate faith and deeds and you end up with a cadaver, a corpse. The truth is, in our world we have a lot of people who only have half living faith. Worse, many have dead faith.

I get up every day, read my devotion, pray to God. But when I step out and am going down the street, I see the need of a neighbor or of a child. I know the need of hunger and know that I have a soup kitchen in my community that needs my help. I feel God prodding me to do something, but I'm still stuck. What has happened is that my faith has become more like a picture on the wall, something I adore and look at but something that doesn't really mean anything.

James says that somebody who does not live into their faith by action is like somebody who walks in the mirror, looks at themselves, and walks away forgetting what they saw. It would be kind of like me getting up in the morning and, seeing that my hair's messed up, I say "Oh well" before walking off. It's like not taking advantage of what I see to change my behavior or my appearance.

As we think about being a person who is taking care of their soul and at the same time trying to listen to the needs, what we have to understand is that one cannot happen without the other. In order to know where I need to go, I need to have a relationship with God. In order for that relationship with God to bear fruit, I have to find a place to share the grace that I'm receiving from my God.

YOUR STORY

What is it you do to take care of your soul?

_____

_____

_____

What is it that you do to take care of your brothers and sisters in this world?

_____

_____

_____

PRAYER PROMPT

Ask God to reveal truth about your weaknesses. Ask to draw close to Him. Ask to bear fruit in order to share from the grace you receive.

DAY 15: SUNDAY

READ SCRIPTURE: JAMES 5:7-11

Early in the church persecution was heavy. The early people began to go underground and hide. Some tried to do the works of Christ, but mostly they were afraid of what would happen to themselves if they really lived into their faith. Most began to just quietly share, and that was all they did.

James challenged them to understand that the faith of Jesus Christ is the faith that makes you step out in your relationship with God, even to the point of the cross. That's what Jesus was about; living in faith and living in action had consequences. To try to avoid those consequences or to not pay enough attention to your faith is detrimental, not only to you but to the people around you.

An old radio is a perfect paradigm for our faith. I can't hold or grasp the radio waves that are coming into the receiver, but what I *can* do is hear the output. It is this invisible faith that produces an audible product. In our everyday life there is this inseparable continuity between getting to know God intimately and God creating within us a desire to do something about it.

When I think about it, in the past, I've mostly been a doer. There's a song that goes along with this text in James that says, "I will not a hearer only be, I will be a doer and then they'll see." Sometimes I've been so busy doing that I haven't taken the time I need to listen and make sure that I'm doing the *right* things.

If we read First Corinthians, Paul talks about the fruit of the spirit of love and says we may die at the stake. I may give my life for the sake of the gospel. I may proclaim beautifully the gospel. But if it's not filled with the agape of God, then the action is empty and it doesn't bear the fruit that God intends it to bear. Therein lies the wonderful paradox of tension of the Christian faith. We are at once receiving God's love and grace, God's edification and direction. But then the whole thing is learning to act on that, to take the instruction, to take the formation and allow it to change our behavior.

YOUR STORY

When has your faith had consequences?

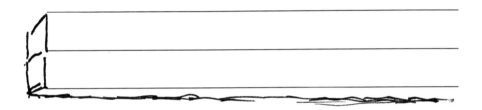

What times in your life have you seen others blessed by the overflow of God in your heart?

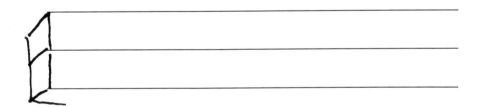

PRAYER PROMPT

Pray for God to teach you how to act on your faith. Ask Him to provide opportunites for you to be the hands and feet of Jesus to a needy world. Thank Him for the wonderful grace we've received.

DAY 16: MONDAY

READ SCRIPTURE: JAMES 3:13-17

Faith communities embody the same disconnect we discussed yesterday. There are some churches that have incredible worship, incredible Bible study and not one single mission outreach.

At the same time there are people and churches that gather together that may feed the poor every week, but the people there have no working knowledge of the scripture and have no idea how to pray.

The truth is both people are underfed, undernourished and underdeveloped. My prayer for you is that you can honestly assess your life, realizing "I'm a lot of action and not enough prayer," or "I'm a lot of prayer and not enough action."

The text in James says what good is it if you walk upon somebody who's freezing to death and you simply offer to pray for them? Well, the truth is I do not know a whole lot of prayers that homeless people can put on and wear to block out freezing weather.

I think back to an experience I had in Philadelphia with the homeless project, *The Paupers Rite of Passage.* After spending a weekend living as the homeless do, I was in those last moments of being out and didn't have a coat. I was wet and cold, and the young woman who had ministered came to a couple of us and said, "You folks need coats." She found coats for my companions, but she couldn't find a coat for me.

She began to apologize profusely. But what was really intriguing about the situation was that she didn't stop there. She stopped right in front of me and began to pray. "Lord, this man needs a coat, help me find a coat." Then, she went back downstairs taking me with her. We went into a storage closet and, sure enough, within minutes she had pulled out a coat.

Faith without works is dead. I would have felt okay if the lady would have just prayed for me and said, "I'm sorry you don't have a coat." But her faith would not let her do that. She knew God was the God of her vision, so she walked back down those stairs after praying and found that coat.

Both of us watched the witness of God's faithfulness in her action. What a gift. It began with her willingness to turn to God and say, "Look, God, I need help. I need help."

The God of intimacy, the God of personal holiness, is the God who is more than willing to come in and give us direction in life. *Thy kingdom come, Thy will be done.* That's the perfect illustration of this tension.

Thy kingdom come is an act of submission. *Thy will be done* is an act of submission. But, *Thy kingdom come, Thy will be done* is also an act of obedience and an act of service. Without that balance, the prayer means nothing. It can't stay in our heart.

YOUR STORY

Who do you know who lives an example of this balance?

_____

PRAYER PROMPT

Thank God for the witness of the individual listed above. Pray for churches and people who put feet on their faith by serving others. Ask God to show you ways to pray more effectively and ways to serve.

DAY 17: TUESDAY

READ SCRIPTURE: MATTHEW 21:21

I want to give you a challenge today. As you look at your faith, how intimate are you with God? Are you practicing your faith inside? Are you talking to God regularly? Are you reading God's Word regularly? Are you allowing that God to bring you the instruction information that will inform your action?

Many people wonder, because they haven't even asked God, what it is He wants them to do. Many people, in the name of Christ, are doing stuff God would never have them do.

Part of our responsibility is in that personal holiness to take responsibility of our relationship with God, like any other relationship, and pay attention to it so that we can learn and be guided into how we should act and live.

I thank God for His patience. I thank God that maybe the Holy Spirit has been stirring in you and challenging you to think about how you live your faith. Maybe He's made you desire to understand that this glorious faith we have not only informs us, but it also leads us into action.

Can we pray together today?

> Dear God, we praise You for Your grace. We give You thanks for Your willingness to become a part of our life. We give You thanks for the fact that you are a personal God, and we know that it is an incredible gift.
>
> But, Father, remind us that the personal relationship is not complete until it turns into obedient action and service of us, Your servants.

Father, there are people reading this today who need their relationship with You strengthened. May Your Holy Spirit brush up against them even now.

But more than that, may they act on that brush and begin to cultivate their relationship with You. Thank You, in Jesus' name. Amen.

I hope you'll go forward in this walk towards Easter striving to be a person who lives and acts on their faith. May you stay in prayer to find the strength and the courage to do that.

YOUR STORY

What things have occupied your time that you suspect are things God has never intended for you?

_____

_____

_____

What actions can you begin today on the path to find out what it is God *does* want you doing?

_____

_____

_____

DAY 18: WEDNESDAY

READ SCRIPTURE: JAMES 1

In our modern-day age, we live in this stressful, work-centered, activity-centered world where *busy*ness is the watch word.

One of the challenges that we encounter when we read the Book of James is finding a way to practice spiritual disciplines- keeping our soul in shape -and also practicing servant disciplines that keep us living into our faith. It is the discipline of exercise. The discipline (hear that word *discipline*) that helps us form and shape how we live.

As much as I love Christ and being a called preacher, finding the ritual of discipline and paying attention to my prayer life is no small task. As a matter of fact, I keep thinking about James wrestling with this whole idea of wisdom. James's definition of *wisdom* was living life well, which meant not just knowing something but knowing how to use it in everyday life. That's the tension of God and Intimacy in Action.

I watch the SuperBowl each year. No matter who you root for, one of the things that strikes me each year is how much these professional football players practice. They're so intent in their practice that some of the teams actually take a "halftime" during practice to get used to the length of halftime during the actual game. They replicate this practice to that degree.

At first, you think it's silly, but the truth is . . . practice makes perfect, right?

YOUR STORY

What does it mean to perfect our practices of the faith?

_____

_____

_____

What are the practices you'd like to start to step up your game?
How can you get accountability and make it happen?

_____

_____

_____

PRAYER PROMPT

Thank God for His order in the universe. Pray for His strength
to know and do the daily disciplines necessary to finish the
game strong. Ask for helpers to be placed in your path who will
encourage and cheer you forward.

DAY 19: THURSDAY

READ SCRIPTURE: MATTHEW 5:20

The founding father of The United Methodist Church, John Wesley, was a brilliant man. An Oxford scholar, he grew up in the Anglican Church where life was centered around inside the walls of these sanctuaries.

Later in life, Wesley went to the United States, visited Georgia, and saw the stark need. Something inside of him let Wesley understand that knowing and studying was not enough. So he began to explore service. Do you know that John Wesley was responsible for the first Campus Ministry? That he was responsible for some of the first hospital ministries? That his work with the poor took him out of those sanctuaries into communities where he felt very uncomfortable?

But he knew he could not stay away because his faith would not let him. In the United Methodist tradition, we have this wonderful struggle of what Wesley called "acts and means of grace" and "acts and means of faith." We are to be about doing mercy works while letting the mercy of God work on us.

Wesley developed into the very DNA of the Wesleyan Movement, the United Methodist Church, the importance of helping people find the balance that they were not only called to *go to church*, they were called to *be the church*.

That's the call we give to you today. There is no Holy reprieve from either personal holiness or social holiness just because you're sick or homebound. That call transcends unhealthy desires. We can't do whatever we want like eating plate after plate at covered dish meals; there is no kind of special dispensation because you've given your life to Christ.

It's the same way in my life in my faith. Many times when I preach, I'll go in and prepare for the sermon. It's my *work*. It did cause me to study scripture. I had to integrate it with the hymns. I had to have conversations with other people. I had to see if it was relevant. But the truth is many times I was not nurturing my soul. I was just getting my sermon done. I thought that because I was doing that kind of work, maybe I was exempt.

Maybe you have some of the same problems. Maybe you think because you're 82 years old you're prayed up. Maybe you think you've done your term. As a pastor, I've heard this again and again and again. "Well, preacher, I've done my stint in the church."

Well, you want to know what? The kingdom is eternal. And I think even after you die, you're not done. And so part of the challenge is discovering that whatever phase of life you're in, you find the balance of continuing to fall in love with the God that made you.

YOUR STORY

How will you go about continuing to seek to please God and live into the life God would have you live by acting upon your faith?

_____

_____

_____

PRAYER PROMPT

Talk to God honestly about whether or not He feels you are still useful. Ask Him to give you opportunities to show your faith. serving others in need.

DAY 20: FRIDAY

READ SCRIPTURE: 2 CORINTHIANS 9: 6-15

One of the gifts I've discovered in my faith is this: *God's kingdom economy is incredible.* We practice reading, praying, public worship and accountability groups, and the practicing of it has value.

The way God has designed this kingdom is that when we invest ourselves in God's Word, that Word, as the scripture says, does not return to us void. It bears something in us. When we do good, it never fails that we are blessed more than the giving. That's just the way this kingdom works.

I find that when I'm disciplined in my faith, I'm alive and vital. God is close. I feel that my faith is vibrant. When I am active in serving, when I go to Nicaragua and look at those children, when I do a *Stop Hunger Now* packing, when I visit one of our community centers and spend time there . . . every one of those times I feel that I'm a part of something that is changing the world.

It affects me. It's not just like I'm pleasing God to keep God from getting mad. It's that I'm receiving these gifts that are not only changing me, they're changing the world.

That's how church is. Ask yourself this: *How am I allowing God to bless me in my spiritual disciplines, and how am I finding ways for God to bless me in my service?*

It's a gift. What a crazy secret! Just like health, when I workout, I get healthier. Imagine that.

So, in this world and in this life, be involved with God intimately and live a life of actions.

YOUR STORY

What makes you feel most healthy spiritually? List the areas where your faith and actions meet to give you that feeling of changing the world.

PRAYER PROMPT

Pray with me:

> *Dear God, thank You that You're patient with us, but more than that, thank You for the genius of Your design in kingdom. That, as we seek to know You, we get to know You, and that as we seek to serve You, we find the joy of being served in our giving.*
>
> *How incredible! Thank You, thank You, thank You, Amen.*

DAY 21: SATURDAY

READ SCRIPTURE: JOHN 4:7-26

There are blood pressure machines that check your health and wellness. It is one of the tools that sees if your heart and blood flow are performing right.

Part of what church does is to help us test our spiritual relationship, our spiritual health. We go to worship and allow the movement of the Holy Spirit, the message of the preacher, and the fellowship and communion of the saints to go to work on our hearts. Sometimes I've gone to church, and, by being there, have taken my spiritual pressure only to realize my soul may be out of sync . . . *I may be out of touch with God.*

Being in that worship service, I get an accurate reading on where I am spiritually. Like the blood pressure cuff that deflates to reveal the upper and lower numbers, hopefully, it lets me know that I'm ok.

One of the best things to help is spending some time in fellowship and sharing special moments with those we love. The things that keep us healthy are our conversations together and the communion we share as children of God. Community makes us better, and that's what God wants for *you*.

If you feel alone, ask God for a friend. If you don't have a church home, ask God to guide you to that place.

Look around your community and find those folks who need a new heart, who need a new spirit, who need a community. Reach out to them and invite them in. Go to their home. Become their friend. Help them take a spiritual pulse, take their spiritual pressure. Help them discover a new life in community.

YOUR STORY

Have you taken your spiritual blood pressure in church lately?
What do the numbers say to you?

_____

_____

_____

Other indicators speak to us. Who are those with which you
associate? Those people and things you spend time on indicate
truths about your heart. Are their changes you need to make for
your health? Describe those here:

_____

_____

_____

PRAYER PROMPT

Prayer is another indicator of health. Are you comfortable praying?
If not, tell that to God. He knows already! All He wants to do is be
in communion with you, to walk with you and talk with you. Tell
Him the concerns, joys and hopes you have on your heart today.

DAY 22: SUNDAY

READ SCRIPTURE: SECOND PETER 1

In this scripture the people don't know how to hear this incredible gift of Jesus Christ. Peter really wrestled with that. Peter had been a fisherman all his life and, at best, was a tangential person of faith. Jesus would quote Isaiah and share His faith as a good Jewish Rabbi. Peter was intrigued by what Jesus had to say.

What fascinated Peter most was that Jesus would talk in language of parables and common examples. Most of the time, in the Bible, when the disciples said they didn't understand it was because they didn't want to hear what was said. It was not that they didn't understand *what* was said.

I think this is the challenge we face in our faith. We live in a world where marketing tells us that everything should taste good, everything should feel good, and everything should add to our pleasure. One of the ironic pieces of the redemption of Jesus Christ is that before we can get better, we really have to kind of get worse.

So when we talk about sharing our faith, nobody really wants to hear, "My chains are gone." That reminds us that we're all chained. We all want to think that we're already free, that we already control our life, and that we really have a good life making all of the decisions.

When we begin to talk to people about faith, we have to begin to find a common language that helps us touch that resonate note that is in all of us; that note that says, "The life I have is not the life I fully want."

There is a yearning in all of us for more; we all have this insatiable hunger that we can't figure out how to satisfy.

71

So how do you discuss that with people in a way that engages them thoughtfully? Bill Hybles, pastor at Willow Creek Church, has written a book called *Walk Across the Room*. For me, it's probably one of the most poignant statements about how we should talk about our faith.

His premise ties right to the title. It is simply this: there are people in your life who need you to just go to them and begin a conversation. They need you to allow the Holy Spirit to be present in that conversation and to trust that the Holy Spirit has already done some work there.

Early in my ministry I carried a brick around my neck: the idea that I had to save people, that it was on me as a preacher to make sure that everybody was on that gospel ship, that everybody's chains were broken, and that everybody knew about amazing grace.

What I found early on is that there were people who didn't want to hear it. There were people who resisted and became angry when I tried to share my Good News with them.

Let me tell you a truth: even if you do this right, some people don't want to receive what you say.

I want you to marinate in that a little bit. This conversation is not about notches in your belt, spiritually. This is about having authentic conversation with people about the quality of their life and about the depth of their relationship. It is about claiming something that's already been promised to them by God that they cannot *have* unless they *accept*. That's just the truth.

PRAYER PROMPT

Ask God to help you find thoughtful ways to talk about your faith.

DAY 23: MONDAY

READ SCRIPTURE: ACTS 2:42-47

Typing here on my iPad, I was thinking about what it means to share the gospel these days. Though the message stays the same, the ways we communicate change almost daily.

When I first began in ministry, phones were hooked to the wall on a cord. If you wanted to have a conversation, you got on the phone, you dialed the number, and you called a person who stood there at the other end.

In that day, the model was neighborhood. Everybody knew their neighbor, mostly, and you actually lived in communities where you could walk to school. I noticed a lot of new subdivisions are trying to revert back to that.

But we live in a very different world than the world of Jesus and the apostles. The good news: we have the same God. How do we take the tools we have today like social media and use them to talk about a God who can change lives?

No matter which delivery message we use, the key is sharing our faith in simple, authentic conversation. The bottom line: you've got nothing to talk about if you've got nothing to talk about. If you don't have a real relationship with God, if God is not at work in your life, and if you're not waking up in the morning engaging the Word or engaging in prayer and having a conversation with God, then it's going to be really difficult to talk to anybody about their life and the possibilities Christ could bring into it.

You can't share your faith unless your faith is vital and alive, unless you have the stories to tell of intersections where Christ has come into your life and helped you find strength.

A relationship with God is something that does not exempt us from the trials of life; rather, it strengthens us for them.

I've talked of how Christ helped me through my quadruple bypass surgery. I've told personal stories of encounters where God has helped make me an answer to somebody else's prayer and vice versa. None of those stories would happen if there wasn't an authentic relationship with Jesus Christ.

YOUR STORY

Explain how your relationship with Christ allows you to talk to others about Him or how your lack of relationship keeps you from being an effective witness:

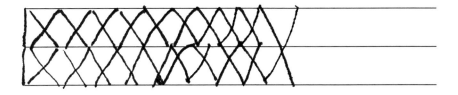

PRAYER PROMPT

Pray with me.

Dear God, as we come to You today, we know that You're just as real as our iPad, that You can answer our questions better than Siri, and that You, through authentic relationship, can give us the opportunity to help people discover new life. Help us to take the time to do that, and to have the courage to trust Your Holy Spirit. All this we lift up in Jesus' name. Amen.

DAY 24: TUESDAY

READ SCRIPTURE: JOHN 12:1-8

The first step to sharing Christ effectively to others on your journey is being alive in your faith. The second step is having relationships with other people.

One of the reasons that we're not being very effective in sharing our faith is very few of us have real, authentic relationships with other people. Relationship means spending time. That doesn't mean you're getting on Facebook and posting inspirational pieces to change people's lives that way. I like some of the stuff that's put on there, but, the truth be told, I don't know of many souls that have been saved by a post on Facebook.

The truth is this has to happen one on one. This has to happen through true relationship, and that takes something that is probably the most precious commodity in our culture: *time.*

If you're too busy, then don't think about being a witness. We are on our devices around five times longer than we spend time with real people. Now, there's something wrong with that picture.

One of the challenges of sharing your faith is to put down the phone, to put down the iPad, to turn off the computer and to walk to a neighbor's house to begin to build a relationship.

Randy Frazee went to a church called Pantego Bible Church in Texas and built a community that was centered around neighborhood and family groups. I spent ten days with Randy and just marveled at the depth of relationship with those people. They were in and out of each other's lives in a very real way.

That Sunday, Randy and I went to worship together. There was a couple having marriage trouble. Their family group leader encouraged them to go down to the communion altar at the end of the service and to allow that group to pray for them.

That is how you share your faith. It is no quick, microwave way. It is through authentic trust and relationship.

Those of us in the church really have to be guardians of our time.

One of the things I preach is simplification. *Slow down and create time to be with each other. Fall in love with each other. Fall in love with God, and enjoy the relationships that lead to the richness of opportunity to share your faith.*

We've got to get outside our walls. We've got to get outside our virtual reality if we're really going to share this faith that changes lives.

YOUR STORY

How much time do you spend with God? How rich is that relationship?

_____

_____

_____

Who do I know well enough to go share the Gospel with them? Who do I need to know better?

_____

_____

_____

PRAYER PROMPT

Pray for your relationship with the Father. Ask His help in giving you the words to say and the opportunities to say them. Sincerely ask for God to strengthen your relationships with others and with Him. Confess those areas where you've come up short in this regard. Lay those things down at His feet and seek a new start in your walk with Him.

DAY 25: WEDNESDAY

READ SCRIPTURE: JOHN 15:16-17

I serve a great church in beautiful Clinton, Mississippi. The city has an area of vintage buildings and quaint shops known as Olde Towne Clinton. There are even brickstreets that are historic and celebrated. Within all of this there is an intentional effort by the landscaping crew that takes care of this Olde Towne area to plant colorful flowers all around. It's done there to beautify this area.

There are vibrant purple and yellow pansies or petunias. I'm not sure what they are called. Whatever they are, they're beautiful and were planted by somebody.

Sometimes we forget that, as people, God chooses us and then plants us to beautify His world. He plants us to use our gifts, our abilities, and our identities to create the garden of life that is so much a part of this world.

The scripture for today is one of my favorites. Eugene Peterson's *The Message* puts it like this: *You didn't choose Me, remember; I chose you. I put you in the world to bear fruit, fruit that won't spoil. As fruit bearers, whatever you ask the Father in relation to Me, He gives you. But remember the root command, love one another.*

We have a ritual almost every spring at our house. We head out to the nursery. We get ready to replant the flowerbeds in the front of our house. We also have window boxes and choose a color or a theme. At the nursery, we go through all the flowers and handpick the ones that we want to put.

God does say I want you, and I have a call for you. But, God not only chooses us; this scripture also tells us that then God has a *place* for us.

How wonderful! God plants us *in a particular place.* God puts us in places where our gifts and graces can be used.

YOUR STORY

What do you like or dislike about the place where you are planted?

_____

_____

_____

God doesn't necessarily ask us to change the whole world. He does, however, expect us to change *our* world, the world around us. In what ways can you take that challenge to heart and really begin to make a bigger difference in the lives of those around you?

_____

_____

_____

PRAYER PROMPT

Pray for God to show you the reasons why He has you planted where you are planted. Ask for the help to blossom and reflect His beauty.

DAY 26: THURSDAY

READ SCRIPTURE: JOHN 19:25-27

I love those brick streets of Clinton, Mississippi. There's just
something different about them. It's not like a layer of asphalt
that was laid out quickly by a machine. That type of craftsmanship
takes people. There is a pattern. They are *down to earth.*

Those streets become a place where this community has an annual
celebration called the *Brick Streets Festival.* It is a place where
people come together around this community they've built. They
enjoy each other.

I think that in the Kingdom of God, what we need to remember is
that life itself is this process of discovering who we are: our identity,
our call, our choseness. It's also discovering how to grow up in
that awareness. Life itself is the growing *into* life, the discovery of
all the facets, the building of relationships, and the development of
community.

That is God's dream for us. He wants us to really live in and grow
up together, finding ourselves strong enough to interrelate and to
find the richness and depth of life.

I wish I would have known sooner that truth. For a long time,
my life was not about growing *into life.* It was about going to a
destination. It was about reaching a certain place. I would find
myself not paying attention to what was going on around me, to
the growth that was happening, to the things that were there. I was
always going someplace else.

Because of that, I missed a lot. I wish we could understand the
power of growing up. I wish we could enjoy the changes in
ourselves, the transformation in our personality, and the increasing

of our mind. That brings God great joy as He watches us when we're planted. He thrills as we become healthy and begin to grow.

YOUR STORY

What are the festivals in your life where you intentionally celebrate community?

_____

_____

_____

What things do you need to be able to grow more beautiful?

_____

_____

_____

PRAYER PROMPT

Spend time today thanking God for the area where you are planted. Be specific in giving thanks for the people around you especially.

DAY 27: FRIDAY

READ SCRIPTURE: MATTHEW 7:16-20

I love bartlett pear trees. They're beautiful, ornamental trees. However, that's the problem with them, in my opinion. They're gorgeous when the leaves change, and they're gorgeous in the spring when they bloom. But it's kind of like the fig tree in the New Testament with Jesus. There's not a pear in the world that's going to come off of that tree. It was bred to be a flowering tree, not to bear fruit.

God loves us. God calls us. God has put us here in a particular place in order to live out our life. We can't forget, though, that part of our design is to bear fruit. *God expects us to bear fruit!*

We have walked around in Olde Towne Clinton for a few days during these devotions. Some of the neat shops there are the fruit of people's lives. In the Leake Street Collection, there's a collection of antiques where a person has invested themselves in beautiful things. In the Wyatt Waters Gallery, there's art that is Wyatt's beautiful vision of what the world looks like, art that grew out of years of nuturing.

Today, the question becomes, "What are we growing? What are we growing into? What are we producing out of our life? What is happening out of living with us?

Are we like the pear tree: ornamental but not bearing fruit? Or are we like the shops in Olde Towne that bloom from intentionality.

PRAYER PROMPT

Pray with me:

Dear God,

We are rooted in Your love. We are shaped by Your love. We are nurtured by Your love. Our prayer is that the fruit of our life will be filled with Your love, and that love will fall into the lives of those around us. We pray that we will get to the root of life and love one another in order that Your kingdom would come, Your will would be done, and that we would all find life abundant.

Thank You, thank You, thank You for this magnificent garden we call life. Thank You for the wonderful way You feed us and grow us in love. Thank You for the chance to share that love.

In Jesus' name, Amen.

DAY 28: SATURDAY

READ SCRIPTURE: JOHN 15:16

I love the popcorn tree. These are some of the most prolific trees you'll ever see. All over them are these little pods that are seeds. If you ever find a popcorn tree in your yard, you'll find that there are thousands of volunteer little popcorn trees growing up out of the ground.

As we think about faith, I am reminded that Jesus said be fruitful and multiply. It wasn't just that we were supposed to have children. It is that we make disciples of Jesus Christ for the transformation of the world.

When you sow your seeds, you are to sow them into the lives of others. God's vision is that something comes of the process.

When we sow our stories of faith in the lives of others, it helps grow faith in *them*.

I'm so thankful that my mom, my dad, and my grandparents, sowed in me the seeds of their faith. It was authentic. I saw it. I heard them pray. I watched them worship. I went with them to do service for Christ.

Because of that, those seeds bore life in me that is Christ-like. As we think about being chosen by God, being planted by God, and being grown by God, let us realize that others come to know God and God's love out of the fruit of our lives.

The root of it all is to love one another. The simple act of loving each other is the sowing of the seeds of God's love into each other's lives. As we live in this magnificent garden where God has chosen to put us, the possibilities of life and eternal life are limitless.

God is a creative genius.   The truth is, the fruit of God is *us*.
We are God's children. We are the ones who God has formed
and shaped. We are fearfully and wonderfully made. We are
empowered to bear the fruit that helps the love of God grow in
others.

What a gift! What a wonder. I thank God for you. I thank God
that you have chosen to get *down to earth* about your faith through
this study.

YOUR STORY

How can you be more fruitful?

_____

_____

_____

Have you ever fully accepted that you are a beautiful child of God?
How can fully understanding this marvel change the way you live
and bloom?

_____

_____

_____

PRAYER PROMPT

Pray to be more fruitful. Thank God for the fruit of others in your life.

DAY 29: SUNDAY

READ SCRIPTURE: 2 CHRONICLES 7:14

One of the decorations we put out at Easter in our house is a small stuffed lamb. The little rascal is snuggly and soft. It has a bowtie and looks stylish. But, you know what? It doesn't have a name.

One of the things that I've found in my life is it's really easy to feed sheep you don't know. It's really easy to throw up a prayer for all the hungry, to throw up a prayer for all the homeless, and to throw up a prayer for all those who are lost.

It's a lot harder to find one lost person, one homeless person, or one person who is in need of companionship. It's harder with a person who has a name. It's harder to pay attention to them, to invest yourself in them, and to feed them.

I've never had a pet lamb, but I have had pet dogs. Growing up, one of the first gifts I ever received was a little long haired, black weenie dog. She was a very funny looking creature. Her name was Lucy.

She was my first friend. I grew up my whole life knowing Lucy. She loved me faithfully. I never fussed about feeding her; I just did it because she was part of the family.

We lived in Greenwood, and our next door neighbors were Jewish. After Sabbath on Saturday, they would invite Lucy over to their house and feed her pancakes. She would go over there to the back step where my neighbors would always set food out.

They did that because they loved us, and they loved her. They knew Lucy and called her by name. She felt comfortable there.

When Jesus says after Easter to "Feed My sheep," it isn't some anonymous, faceless sheep. Jesus knew that in Peter's life there were people with names. There were people like Peter's brother who he followed to faith. There were people in Peter's life like his cousins, his family, his mother, and his mother-in-law. They are all part of this Gospel story. They are all sheep that Jesus had entrusted to Peter.

As Peter accepted the call into ministry after the resurrection and stepped center stage, guess what? The sheep he was entrusted with were the Gentiles, those people who lived outside the Jewish faith.

Along with Paul, Peter accepted a whole flock of people different than himself because that's where Jesus was leading.

I'm a firm believer that Jesus gives us all sheep whenever we come to faith. There are people in our lives to whom we are to feed the gospel. There are people in our lives to whom maybe we are to feed literally.

What are we feeding them? Let us strive to feed them the love of God, the presence of our spirit and whatever else they need in order that they might live loved.

YOUR STORY

Name the pets from your life. Describe the joy you felt in taking care of them.

_____

_____

_____

_____

Do you allow yourself to feel that same joy in taking care of other
people around you? How can you allow yourself to enjoy the
freedom of spirit it takes to give yourself away, to "feed My sheep"?

_____

_____

_____

PRAYER PROMPT

*Dear God, for Your love we are fed. We are given Your love to feed
others. Lead us to the ones who we can call by name and feed in Your
name, Amen.*

DAY 30: MONDAY

READ SCRIPTURE: EPHESIANS 1:15-23

Paul says the best weapon we have is each other. Sheep have to flock together. It is a defense mechanism. In their weakness, numbers do matter.

So many of you are isolated. Some of you are at home, by yourself. You have a caregiver. Some of you are loners who, even right now, may be sitting in a hotel room, by yourself, away from the people that are there.

You need the weapon of finding people who care about you.

The cool thing about the church is this: even if you're somebody on the road traveling from place to place, there are churches everywhere you go. There are Christians everywhere you are, communities of faith who are about the same kind of life as you.

Don't miss the opportunity to have them. If you're homebound, there are communities around you. Maybe the community you grew up in has disappointed you, maybe that's why you're not there.

There are others. Find a body of Christ. So that together, you're not a loner out trying to do guerilla warfare against odds that outnumber you.

You need other people.

Paul said you need the power of salvation. You need to know that God loves you and wants you alive. God wants you *alive*.

And so He gives you these weapons to protect you, to surround you. He tries to coach you into how to use them. God wants you to wake up every day saying, "I'm a child of God."

You remember the little Bible school song, *I'm in the Lord's Army?* That's who we are. We have an army of believers, not an army who runs into battle to hurt other people. One of the most amazing images of this when Jesus was being betrayed. He was in the garden, and Peter draws his sword. Peter whacks off the ear of one of the people who are there, and Jesus doesn't say, "Go get them, guys!" He picks up the guy's ear. He places it back. He heals it.

Jesus turns to the disciples and says, "This is not how we fight." It's kind of counter-intuitive, but it works. It changed the man whose ear was healed. It changed those who watched. It changed the course of history.

So the weapons God gives are not the weapons of the world. I want to be as blunt as I can be. A lot of people who call themselves Christians do not use or fight with the weapons of faith. They fight with the weapons of the enemy. They seek to take life. They seek to destroy life. They seek to break down life.

You know the truth is that if it smells like a wolf, it probably is a wolf.

So as Christians, we have to create a culture that relies on different weapons.

YOUR STORY

Sticking together is a powerful weapon in fighting the adversary. Who are the people in your life that you know will always have your back- who care and love you?

DAY 31: TUESDAY

READ SCRIPTURE: EPHESIANS 6:10-18

On the battlefield, the first, most important thing is established communication. Let command take control. Prayer is our command and control. It is our establishing communication so that God, through the Holy Spirit, can speak to our spirit and help us make our decisions, help us choose our allies, help us come together and be on our mission. Without prayer and prayer for each other, it's almost impossible to resist the powers of the enemy.

When I find myself struggling spiritually, it is when instead of being a person of the Lord's Army, I withdraw into myself as a survivalist.

You know, I never cease to be amazed at the TV specials showing these people who dig bunkers and fill them with all kinds of food. They pull inside of the bunkers and try to live there, waiting for the end of the earth.

That's not what we were made for. We were made to live life. We're on a journey, and our life is full of attacks as we're on the journey. Bands of rebels and enemies are everywhere, and they are trying to keep us from getting to the land where we're headed.

We have to have prayer to guide us through all of these things, and we have to be with each other in order to be protected.

You know, the other thing that God has given us that we can take anywhere we want is our Word of God, the Bible.

I had a great conversation with Tony Campolo, who wrote a book called *Red Letter Christians*. Tony says that if we as Christians would just take those red letters that are in our Bibles and write them on our hearts and live into them, then we would then truly be Christians, truly help the Kingdom come and God's will be done.

You can have a Bible. You can read it. You can take those red letters and write them on your heart. There *is* power in the blood, and that blood comes from the living Word of God.

That's an incredible weapon. God has given us so much to fight the battles of life, to fight any kind of enemy we encounter. I hope you take advantage of them.

You are not in this by yourself. Know that others are there with you. It's our desire to be a part of that army with you. Let's have a word of prayer as we pray into this.

> *Dear God, we do indeed live among powers and principalities. It seems every day there's more bad news than good. But quietly, through the middle of all the warfare, You're leading your people to You, to the kingdom, to the Promised Land.*
>
> *Let us be a part of one of those ragtag bands. Let us take up the power of prayer, the power of Your scripture, the power of fellowship and the power of the blood of Your salvation. Let us walk bravely as You lead us into battle. In Jesus' name. Amen.*

I hope maybe something I said struck you. Read over the scripture and think about the tools God has given you to fight. Begin to ask yourself, how do I learn to use them?

And remember that the most incredible weapon we have is the gift of love.

YOUR STORY

Spend time with your loved ones exploring that gift of love.

DAY 32: WEDNESDAY

READ SCRIPTURE: JOHN 1:1-5

Sometimes, as we go into Easter, we whiz through the Holy Week stories, the time before the resurrection. We forget how messy and dirty our faith is and how patient and graceful and powerful our God is to enter into that world only to exit through resurrection.

Today's scripture is John's big picture of moving towards Easter.

> *In the beginning was the Word and the Word was with God and the Word was God. He was in the beginning with God, all things were made through Him and without Him, nothing was made that was made. In Him was life and the life was the light of men. And the light shines in the darkness, and the darkness did not comprehend it.*

I never cease to be amazed as to what a poor marketing job Christianity has done for itself. When in the world do you begin a book about faith that says *what we wanted to happen, people didn't understand.*

The light came into the darkness and the darkness comprehended it not.

One of the things John tries to do in his Gospel is to remind us that we live in a world that is messy. There's light ,and there is darkness. There is life, and there is death. There is creation, and there is destruction. There is godliness, and there's ungodliness.

Sometimes in the midst of the world, that messiness makes us wonder what relevance faith has. And it's at that very point that our Christian faith becomes relevant, in the fact that it's not sterilized or cleaned up.

101

There's story after story in the Gospel of disappointment alongside the miracles. Story after story of people who breached their faith as well as those who are faithful.

Moving towards the climax of the crucifixion of Jesus Christ and the resurrection that follows, we are reminded that sometimes good friends can betray good friends, that people can lie and cheat and steal.

And yet there's a common theme that runs through the scripture that serves as our ray of hope. That theme is that regardless of what we do, God's action is unchanging. There's an unswerving commitment by the One who made us and created us to pursue us throughout eternity.

Now did you hear that? I want you to listen to that again. There's an unswerving commitment by the God who made us, to continually enter into that darkness, regardless of whether the darkness understands it or not.

What a promise!

YOUR STORY
Does the world see that light in you? Explain why or why not:

_____

_____

_____

PRAYER PROMPT
Spend time thanking God and praising Him for continually being that light that enters our darkness. Ask for help with those times when you don't remember or understand or claim that light, that hope.

DAY 33: THURSDAY

READ SCRIPTURE: ROMANS 8:31-38

There was a young man who had extraordinary battles with alcohol and drugs. He'd been thrown out by his family. The young man found himself in a group home where he alienated all the house parents and had a terrible reputation.

However, when you got to know the young man, you saw that underneath was pain, hurt, and lack of any kind of hope in the midst of the life he lived. His father had used him. His brother had given up on him. His mother- who knows? He was the perfect picture of darkness.

Yet, every time I would come he knew I was a preacher. I would spend time in that group home as part of my placement and my field work for social work. He would meet me at the door to argue, meet me at the door to vent his anger, but he always met me at the door.

That story reminds me of this, in the midst of our brokenness, there is something underneath us all that yearns for the kind of love that this God seeks to give us. In the midst of our brokenness, in the midst of our capacity to disappoint, in the midst of our ability to hurt other people and to even hurt ourselves, I think there is something innate within us that hungers for something different.

I'd like to tell you that young man came to Jesus under my guidance, but you want to know the truth? He didn't. He was as cynical as he could be as long as I knew him. But, you know what? He kept meeting me. He kept coming and having conversation.

I wonder where he is in his life. And part of the reason I would wonder about him is because of the story that we read in scripture. A story of a timeless pursuit of a God who refuses to give up on an unfaithful people. It is a God who is willing to do anything within His power to make sure that the children He created find their way home.

As we think about the crucifixion and the capacity of human beings, as we turn on the TV and we watch the relentless barrage of people blowing people up around the world, we still see that the darkness doesn't comprehend what we have to say.

Why would we keep saying it? Why would we keep pushing? Why would we even make the effort?

Well, the truth is this. Every once in a while something does change. And regardless of whether we're fruitful or not, I am a firm believer that the God who made us never ever gives up on us all the way through eternity.

One of my favorite songs of all time is from *Man of La Mancha*, "To Dream the Impossible Dream." One of the reasons I love that song is because there's an image in it that we in the Christian community have kind of thrown to the side. There are the words about being willing to march into hell for a heavenly cause, to dream the impossible dream, to fight the unbeatable foe.

There is an element within the Gospel that is relentless in its engagement of what seems to be impossible.

So as we come into these dark times the light of Jesus Christ shines into it. We find that, in spite of the rejection, in spite of the betrayal, in spite of the beatings, in spite of the crown of thorns, Jesus keeps getting up.

Even on the cross, when people don't understand, Jesus is not cursing them, is not giving up, other than giving His ghost to God. He is saying, *Father forgive them, for they know not what they do.*

YOUR STORY

Are you really making a difference? Can we as Christians in this world of darkness really make any difference?

What amazing things does God have in store for you if He was willing to go to such lengths to pursue you? What would you do for Christ if you could achieve anything?

PRAYER PROMPT

Thank God for His faithfulness. Repent of unbelief. Specifically pray for those in your life who need to know, who need to truly believe in the grace and freedom of Christ.

DAY 34: FRIDAY

READ SCRIPTURE: JOHN 3:16-21

So as we prepare for Easter, I want you to begin to ask some questions about your life. Is there cynicism in you? Has the darkness found its way into your heart?

Much of depression is the darkness wrapping itself around us and slowly squeezing the hope out of our life, shrinking our worlds and allowing us not to even begin to comprehend any possibility of hope or escape. The Gospel message reminds us that just because we don't understand the light, it does not mean the light is not there. Just because we don't allow the grace of God to affect us does not mean the grace of God stops *trying* to affect us.

I want you to marinate in that a little bit. God has promised us from the beginning of time that God will be our God and that He will look at us as His people.

What an incredible promise! In good and bad times, in light and dark times, we have been given a promise by God who made and shaped us, that regardless of what we understand or don't understand, God will relentlessly pursue us.

As we make our way towards the cross and we're talking about the messiness of faith, I want you to turn your attention again to yourself. And then I want you to look at the world around you. When you wake up in the morning, what's the spirit that you have? Is it a *woe is me* spirit? Is it a spirit of *I would just as soon not be here?* Is it a spirit of despair?

Maybe it's even worse than that. Maybe it's a spirit of bitterness and anger that says *who deserves this kind of life? I'm home, I'm suffering, I'm hurting, I'm home and nobody cares for me and I don't know what to do about it. People have let me down. The church, the place that is supposed to be the bearer of light, seems to be nothing but a bunch of hypocrites. They don't even get it.*

Well, let me tell you something. Jesus knew they wouldn't get it. Jesus knows we'll never fully understand. And that's why we live by faith.

We have a God who will not give up on us.

That is the whole key of our belief. That God will never, ever, ever give up on us, no matter how messy things get, no matter how unfaithful we are. God is relentless in that pursuit and was willing to become flesh, get dirty, and get into this world to be with us. He came and lived with us until we killed Him.

And even then . . . *even then*, He didn't give up. He came back, resurrected and renewed the mission and the effort to bring light in the darkness, even knowing the darkness would not understand.

Sometimes, I hear people say if you just had the right theology, if you just knew the right things. You know what? I kind of laugh at that.

The bottom line is this. The only thing that's required of faith is faith, to try to believe one thing: God loves us and will never give up, regardless of how dark this world gets.

PRAYER PROMPT

Spend time today thanking God for never giving up on us.

DAY 35: SATURDAY

Did you ever buy a book and flip to the back to read the last words in the last chapter, just to kind of see the ending?

Well here's the ending of our story, the book of Revelation. It is this beautiful image of God building a city, not out of brick and mortar, but out of God's very spirit. All the ends of the earth are gathered into the light of it. That is what we're all walking towards, even now, when we can't see the light.

So I have a question. Do you live your life as if there will never be any light? Or do you live your life as if even in the darkness, the light will one day come?

That's the people we are, the people who understand that darkness is not a myth but real. We also believe with all our heart and soul that the light will come. In fact, that light is with us now.

My prayer as you move towards Easter is that somewhere in your life the Holy Spirit will move and awaken within you a sense of hope. I pray God will give you a sense of joy of knowing that neither life nor death, nor powers nor principalities, nor things present, nor things past can separate you from the relentless pursuit of the God who loves you!

For me, I need to hear that. Even more, I pray I can live into it.

That's the Easter prayer for you. In some way, I pray you will believe that the light is coming in the darkness, even if you can't understand it.

YOUR STORY

What do you feel when hearing that "neither life nor death, nor powers nor principalities, nor things present, nor things past can separate you from the relentless pursuit of the God who loves you"? What confidence and freedom should that give you daily?

_____

_____

_____

_____

PRAYER PROMPT

Pray with me:

Dear God, for Your relentless, unswerving faith in us, we give You thanks. Forgive our unbelief and renew our hearts that the day will come when we are part of the light that comes into the darkness, even when people don't understand it. In Jesus name we pray, Amen.

DAY 36: PALM SUNDAY

READ SCRIPTURE: LUKE 22:7-38

Today is Palm Sunday, a day that reminds us that we are a crazy people full of passion, full of fear. We are entering into this season, the high season in the Christian church year, called Holy Week. We start with Palm Sunday. You probably remember the story of Jesus' procession into the city. People lined the path waving palm branches, calling Him king. It was the beginning of the most tumultuous week in the history of faith, a time that was full of high highs and low lows.

When we're talking about the reality of Holy Week, the truth is that our scripture does not sterilize the road to the cross and the resurrection. Rather, it accentuates the humanness, the emotion, the passion that's associated with the craziness of living in this world. It's a world where emotion and passion are not only real they're palpable. Jesus lived in this world.

Let's walk into Holy Week by turning to the Gospel of Luke. Eugene Peterson tells this story of the Passover meal, and I think it vividly shows the volatility of life, how God deals with it, and how we deal with it.

> When it was time, He sat down, all the apostles with Him, and said, you've no idea how much I have looked forward to eating this Passover meal with you before I enter my time of suffering. It's the last one I'll eat until we all eat it together in the kingdom of God.
>
> Taking the cup, He blessed it, then said, take this and pass it among you. As for Me, I'll not drink wine again until the kingdom of God arrives.

*Taking bread, He blessed it, broke it, and gave it to them,
saying, this is My body, given for you. Eat it in My memory.
He did the same with the cup after supper, saying, this cup
is the new covenant written in my blood, blood poured out
for you.*

*Do you realize that the hand of the one who is betraying
Me is at this moment on this table? It's true that the Son of
Man is going down a path already marked out, no surprises
there. But for the one who turns Him in, turns traitor to the
Son of Man, this is doomsday.*

*They immediately became suspicious of each other and
began quizzing one another, wondering who might be about
to do this.*

*Within minutes they were bickering over who would do this,
how it would end up, who would be the greatest.*

*But Jesus intervened: Kings like to throw their weight
around and people in authority like to give themselves fancy
titles. It's not going to be that way with you. Let the senior
among you become like the junior; let the leader act the part
of the servant.*

*Who would you rather be: the one who eats the dinner or
the one who serves the dinner? The one, would you rather
eat and be served, right?*

*But I've taken My place among you as the one who serves.
And you've stuck with Me through thick and thin. Now
I confer on you the royal authority My Father that He
conferred on Me so you can eat and drink at My table
in My kingdom and be strengthened as you take up
responsibilities among the congregations of God's people.*

YOUR STORY

What is God saying to you in this passage of scripture?

PRAYER PROMPT

Our journey is winding down. God has revealed many truths to us in a real, earthy way. Get real with God confessing those areas where we concentrate on the palm branches rather than on the Christ. Ask God to reveal Himself to you and to your church during this special Holy Week.

DAY 37: MONDAY

READ SCRIPTURE: JOHN 12:12-19

The whole story of Holy Week begins with palm branches. Before we can get to the Maundy Thursday table, there's this parade. There's this joyous, ecstatic celebration. I think many times we don't quite understand this. The people of Israel had been waiting for a savior for generations. Even the possibility that that was going to happen stirred energy and also fear at a lot of levels. Sometimes, as we plunge into this story, the images of the palm branches are what capture us, not the images of the emotion; but the emotion had to be thick.

I wonder what it is that Jesus is feeling as He rides in on that donkey. That's the piece that I feel like we strip away from this story. Jesus was fully human. He felt. He looked around as he rode past all the cheering crowd. Jesus knows that the cross is where He's headed.

It had to be like a bone that stuck in his craw. *Here they are, laying down their garments, throwing the palm branches. Here are the cheers and joy. And yet so soon they'll be asking Me to be killed.*

Sometimes, instead of the palm branch imagery, it is so helpful to us to find images that help us unsterilize the gospel, that help us feel the passion and the emotion and the reality of how our life in faith is messy.

My good friend, Anthony Thaxton, produced an incredible book, *Stations of the Cross*. The book tells the passion story and takes us through the movements of Jesus through artwork. Those images help capture in my imagination, the realness of this moment. The style Anthony used just really awakens emotions. It is that kind of splattering that reminds us of how messy life is, how real life can be.

Passion Week reminds us of our passion and also of our fickleness. Jesus has gathered everybody at the table and says, "I hope you hear these words: I've waited a long time for this; this is our last meal together."

Do you feel the emotion in that? These men who had followed Him, had been so close together, were now gathered listening. Jesus looks around the table and has to say, "One of you is going to sell Me out."

Wow. What a moment to experience. How critical this time was. Jesus is dealing with His emotions- the emotion of loss, the emotion of His love for the disciples, the emotion of the disappointment of Judas betraying Him.

Instead of Jesus giving the disciples a lecture about what they should have done, about how wrong they were, Jesus loved them. Instead of calling Judas out and having the disciples dish out their justice, Jesus took a towel and washed their feet. Jesus looked at them and said, "The gift I want to leave you is that this kingdom is not going to be like you think."

Jesus tried to teach them this all along: things in His kingdom are upside down.

Their emotion was fickle. They had passion and wanted to go to war to bring a kingdom into power. They wanted to know who would be in power, who would sit at the right or the left.

Jesus said, "That is not what I'm here for."

YOUR STORY

Do you try to make Christ into your image rather than letting it be the other way around? How can you avoid putting Him into a box?

_____

_____

_____

What message is Jesus still trying to get us understand today?

_____

_____

_____

PRAYER PROMPT

Ask God to help you not miss the moments where He shows Himself this week. Pray for His clarity for purpose in your life.

DAY 38: TUESDAY

READ SCRIPTURE: MARK 9:33-37

Jesus wanted the passion of the disciples to not be in the ordinary places of power and control; instead, Jesus wanted a kingdom of *service*.

Jesus told the disciples, "What I've tried to teach you since I've been with you is that I came to serve, to love, to heal, to reconcile, and not to destroy."

We think, how could the disciples not get it? But, we turn around and act the same way. So many times when we get caught up in the emotion of our lives, when we're caught up in the pain of the world, our first reaction is to run away like Peter. When we see each other disappointed, we choose to fight.

Jesus says neither is right. We humble ourselves and we become obedient to God. We serve.

And so Jesus, looking at His disciples, said, "I know you can't understand this, but when all is said and done, the last will be first. Those of you who want power will have to give it up to really get it."

I read these words and think, *If I'd had heard that, I'd have fallen to my knees and said, "God, what do I need to do?"* But in my heart I know that's not true. I would have done the same thing the disciples did. I wouldn't have dwelt on the truth Jesus spoke, but would've tried to figure out who it was that would betray him. I would think, *there's somebody in this room that's selling him out.* I know that's where my imagination would go. I would be caught up in that gossip that ran around the table. *Is it me? Is it me? Wait till we get our hands on him. We can't believe there's somebody like that*

122

among us. That's exactly what happened in that room. Jesus lost them, and their emotions took over.

YOUR STORY

We've all betrayed Christ. What are some of those times (even though you'd really like to forget them)?

_____

_____

_____

_____

When and where do your emotions get the better of you? What can you do about those times?

_____

_____

_____

_____

PRAYER PROMPT

Pray for forgiveness in those times we've just really messed things up. Ask for the strength to forgive yourself and for the courage to lay those things down and leave them at the cross.

DAY 39: WEDNESDAY

READ SCRIPTURE: LUKE 22:7-38

As the Last Supper concludes, notice how this scripture ends. Jesus just has to say, "We've got to go; it's time."

I think that Jesus recognized that there before Him was the drama of humanity. On display was our vulnerability, our lack of ability to stay on task, our sin which is always so prevalent. And rather than being disgusted, what I really think happened was that Jesus understood better than ever the necessity of going to the cross.

Passion Week. The craziness of our lives as humans. How in the world can people start with Palm Sunday and end with the crucifixion? In just one week's time, we go from calling Jesus "King" to yelling, "Crucify Him!"

It still seems so unbelievable to us. But I've done the same thing in my life. When my grandfather died, it was one of the most emotional times in my life. I can remember being that teenager so close to God one week, and (after hearing of my grandfather's death) railing all the way to Oklahoma, asking, "What kind of God lets a grandfather die?" I couldn't believe God was that mean. I couldn't believe God was that hateful.

We have such short memories. We have such volatile emotions. We have such poor control over who we are.

But the good news is this: God doesn't. What if God reacted emotionally like us? Do you understand how many times He'd have had to recreate this world? How many floods there would have been? How many storms there would have been? How many times He would've had to wipe the map clean to start over?

Thankfully that's not how God operates. God has, from the very beginning of time, overcome our fickleness with His faithfulness. He comes at us, even in the midst of a cross, not with retaliation but with resurrection. He brings a hope of life, a beautiful forgiveness, a brand new beginning.

For me, that's the story of this Holy Week. It is not that we're so totally messed up. It's a wonderful God intent on loving us and calling us to Him.

YOUR STORY

Who is the person in your life who most exemplies the spirit of Christ?

_____

What can you learn from that person?

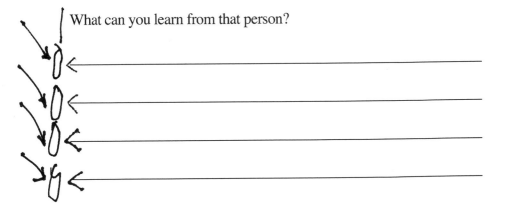

_____

_____

_____

_____

PRAYER PROMPT

Ask God to mold you into His likeness. Pray for a narrowing of focus in your world to the things that truly matter. Pray specifically by name for those in your sphere of influence asking for God's direction in how you can better serve them.

DAY 40: MAUNDY THURSDAY

READ SCRIPTURE: LUKE 22:39-65

My prayer for you as you get ready for Easter is that somehow you would receive that gift of grace and hear those words of Jesus: "I don't know what you expect from this kingdom, but I am here to serve you; I want to teach you how to live a life like that, where you're not run by emotion but by faith."

Are you mad at God? *He can handle it.*

Are you broken? *He can handle it.*

Are you waiting for a Savior? *He can handle it.*

But maybe not in the way you would think.

> *Dear God, we thank You for the images that kindle within us, the messiness of this life. We thank You for the honesty of the Gospel that doesn't polish up a story and try to make things look cleaner and neater than they were.*
>
> *We are messy. We are sinful. We are broken and yet You still wash our feet. You love us. You vie for us. You come back for us.*
>
> *Thank you; let us live into that gift in Jesus' name. Amen.*

The heart of the Gospel is that the love of God never goes away.

YOUR STORY

Where are you with God?

_____

_____

_____

_____

Where would you like to be?

_____

_____

_____

_____

PRAYER PROMPT

Pray for God's help in your continuing journey. Ask for God to place people in your life who are able to help you on your way. Ask to be used of God to help others.

Good Friday

LUKE 23 COMMON ENGLISH BIBLE

JESUS BEFORE PILATE

23 The whole assembly got up and led Jesus to Pilate and 2 began to accuse him. They said, "We have found this man misleading our people, opposing the payment of taxes to Caesar, and claiming that he is the Christ, a king."

3 Pilate asked him, "Are you the king of the Jews?" Jesus replied, **"That's what you say."**

4 Then Pilate said to the chief priests and the crowds, "I find no legal basis for action against this man."

5 But they objected strenuously, saying, "He agitates the people with his teaching throughout Judea—starting from Galilee all the way here."

JESUS BEFORE HEROD

6 Hearing this, Pilate asked if the man was a Galilean. 7 When he learned that Jesus was from Herod's district, Pilate sent him to Herod, who was also in Jerusalem at that time. 8 Herod was very glad to see Jesus, for he had heard about Jesus and had wanted to see him for quite some time. He was hoping to see Jesus perform some sign. 9 Herod questioned Jesus at length, but Jesus didn't respond to him. 10 The chief priests and the legal experts were there, fiercely accusing Jesus. 11 Herod and his soldiers treated Jesus with contempt. Herod mocked him by dressing Jesus in elegant clothes and sent him back to Pilate. 12 Pilate and Herod became friends with each other that day. Before this, they had been enemies.

JESUS AND BARRABAS

13 Then Pilate called together the chief priests, the rulers, and the people. 14 He said to them, "You brought this man before me as one who was misleading the people. I have questioned him in your presence and found nothing in this man's conduct that provides a legal basis for the charges you have brought against him. 15 Neither did Herod, because Herod returned him to us. He's done nothing that deserves death. 16 Therefore, I'll have him whipped, then let him go."

18 But with one voice they shouted, "Away with this man! Release Barabbas to us." (19 Barabbas had been thrown into prison because of a riot that had occurred in the city, and for murder.)

20 Pilate addressed them again because he wanted to release Jesus.

21 They kept shouting out, "Crucify him! Crucify him!"

22 For the third time, Pilate said to them, "Why? What wrong has he done? I've found no legal basis for the death penalty in his case. Therefore, I will have him whipped, then let him go."

23 But they were adamant, shouting their demand that Jesus be crucified. Their voices won out. 24 Pilate issued his decision to grant their request. 25 He released the one they asked for, who had been thrown into prison because of a riot and murder. But he handed Jesus over to their will.

ON THE WAY TO THE CROSS

26 As they led Jesus away, they grabbed Simon, a man from Cyrene, who was coming in from the countryside. They put the cross on his back and made him carry it behind Jesus. 27 A huge crowd of people followed Jesus, including women, who were mourning and wailing for him. 28 Jesus turned to the women and

said, "Daughters of Jerusalem, don't cry for me. Rather, cry for yourselves and your children. 29 The time will come when they will say, 'Happy are those who are unable to become pregnant, the wombs that never gave birth, and the breasts that never nursed a child.' 30 Then they will say to the mountains, 'Fall on us,' and to the hills, 'Cover us.' 31 If they do these things when the tree is green, what will happen when it is dry?"

JESUS ON THE CROSS

32 They also led two other criminals to be executed with Jesus. 33 When they arrived at the place called The Skull, they crucified him, along with the criminals, one on his right and the other on his left. 34 Jesus said, **"Father, forgive them, for they don't know what they're doing."** They drew lots as a way of dividing up his clothing.

35 The people were standing around watching, but the leaders sneered at him, saying, "He saved others. Let him save himself if he really is the Christ sent from God, the chosen one."

36 The soldiers also mocked him. They came up to him, offering him sour wine 37 and saying, "If you really are the king of the Jews, save yourself." 38 Above his head was a notice of the formal charge against him. It read "This is the king of the Jews."

39 One of the criminals hanging next to Jesus insulted him: "Aren't you the Christ? Save yourself and us!"

40 Responding, the other criminal spoke harshly to him, "Don't you fear God, seeing that you've also been sentenced to die? 41 We are rightly condemned, for we are receiving the appropriate sentence for what we did. But this man has done nothing wrong." 42 Then he said, "Jesus, remember me when you come into your kingdom."

43 Jesus replied, **"I assure you that today you will be with me in paradise."**

44 It was now about noon, and darkness covered the whole earth until about three o'clock, 45 while the sun stopped shining. Then the curtain in the sanctuary tore down the middle. 46 Crying out in a loud voice, Jesus said, **"Father, into your hands I entrust my life."** After he said this, he breathed for the last time.

47 When the centurion saw what happened, he praised God, saying, "It's really true: this man was righteous." 48 All the crowds who had come together to see this event returned to their homes beating their chests after seeing what had happened. 49 And everyone who knew him, including the women who had followed him from Galilee, stood at a distance observing these things.
Jesus' burial

50 Now there was a man named Joseph who was a member of the council. He was a good and righteous man. 51 He hadn't agreed with the plan and actions of the council. He was from the Jewish city of Arimathea and eagerly anticipated God's kingdom. 52 This man went to Pilate and asked for Jesus' body. 53 Taking it down, he wrapped it in a linen cloth and laid it in a tomb carved out of the rock, in which no one had ever been buried. 54 It was the Preparation Day for the Sabbath, and the Sabbath was quickly approaching. 55 The women who had come with Jesus from Galilee followed Joseph. They saw the tomb and how Jesus' body was laid in it, 56 then they went away and prepared fragrant spices and perfumed oils. They rested on the Sabbath, in keeping with the commandment.

Holy Saturday

All hope seems gone.

Jesus is nowhere to be seen.

Earth is dark.

His followers are scared.

They feel as though they've lost their purpose.

Had times like that in your journey?

Are you in that darkness now, waiting for some ray of hope?

Is someone you know lost in the night?

There is Good News. Joy comes in the morning. . .

Pray for those who feel as though God has disappeared. Pray that though they can't see Him, that doesn't mean He's not fighting for them, loving them, ever drawing to them. Pray for strength in your walk when things seem too *DOWN TO EARTH*.

Pray to always remember that things don't end in that tomb. . .

Easter Sunday

Happy Easter! *Christ is risen!*

Across the world today churches will be full. In fact, on Easter particularly, even those who haven't been to church in a very long time tend to come around. The question is, *why?*

Churches will be full because people are looking for Jesus. People looked for Jesus all through scripture. People have been looking for Jesus since the beginning of time.

Where will we ever find Him? Where is Jesus? Where do you find Jesus in a world that is as messed up as ours?

The Easter story tells us.

Think about what it was like for Mary to come to that empty tomb, to get to that place where she had gone to do her duty as a friend. She went to take care of the body of Jesus. She walks up, looking. He wasn't there.

It's the account from the Gospel of John. Mary comes to the tomb early. She stood outside the tomb weeping. She knelt to look inside the tomb. There was no Jesus inside. Instead sat two angels in white where Jesus' body had been. Gently they asked, "Woman, why do you weep?"

Mary said, "They took my Master, and I don't know where they've put Him."

Then Mary turned away and saw a man standing there. Mary didn't recognize him. The amazing thing, the miraculous thing, is that this man was Jesus.

"Woman, why are you weeping?" Jesus asked. "Who are you looking for?"

Mary, in her grief, thought he was the gardener. She said, "Mister, if you took him, tell me where He is so I can care for His body."

Jesus then called her by her name, "Mary." Turning to face Jesus, she said, "Rabboni!" which meant "teacher" in Hebrew.

What a cool story! Mary loved Jesus as deeply as anybody can love anybody. Her heart was absolutely broken. She had gone to the tomb to pay her last respects and to make sure Christ's body had been cared for. She didn't care what anybody thought.
She didn't care about the political fallout of the crucifixion. All she cared about was looking after Jesus. And when she gets there, Jesus is gone.

I've often wondered what it would be like to go to a funeral of a friend and walk up to the casket to find there's no body in it.

Think about the emotions and the logic that would run to it. You're not going to immediately think, "Oh well, he's resurrected." In fact, the first thought is probably to wonder whether or not this is a joke. Did they forget to put the body inside the tomb? Our very human minds immediately rush to the logic, and that is what happened with Mary. Who took Him? How disrespectful can things get? She's angry. She doesn't care that anybody knows she's angry.

As I read that, it just came to me that our life is spent looking for Jesus. A lot of people go to church, show up every Sunday trying to find Him. They want a savior.

Others go to the bar every Saturday night; they look for Him at the bottom of a cup or a glass. There are people who are looking for life and salvation and a form of Jesus in relationships and money and a thousand things. They go with the highest of expectations.

What happens when they arrive? He's not there.

I talk a lot about churchianity. I speak about how we as religious people many times lose our way. We look for the wrong things in the wrong places. It's well intentioned. It's logical. It's just like Mary. It's her responsibility to go care for the body of Jesus.

But you know what she forgot? Jesus had already told her He wasn't going to be there. He had told the disciples multiple times. "I must die and be resurrected. I must die and be resurrected."

But you know what? They're like us. They had a hard time believing stuff like that. Dead people don't just up and walk out. Life doesn't work like that.

And here's where I really had my heart grabbed because it struck too close to home. The truth is Mary was there because she loved Jesus, not because she believed He'd be resurrected.

Her relationship with Jesus was not about the theology. It was about the man. It was real. It was down to earth. So when she came and found that his body was not there, it rocked her world.

I'm going to be blunt with you. I think many of us fall in love with our faith because we think Jesus was a good guy. We like the way He treats people. We love the wise things He says. But to be honest, this resurrection thing doesn't make any sense. The truth is, most of us would love being a Christian just because of the stories of Jesus.

But you want to know what? That's why we had the resurrection, because this is not just a story of Jesus. This is a story of a God who refuses to let anything get between Him and His people, including our own sinfulness. God will not allow that to separate us from Him. Even if He had to come down and walk among us.

And so as Mary is looking to find the physical body of Jesus, she comes across this gardener. The gardener seems oblivious to what's going on, but no, He's not. He's not really the gardener.

Something's happened. Jesus is different. He has taken on a different form, a different shape. He's in transition. In the spiritual realm, He's not just flesh and blood anymore. The true spirit is blossoming into this eternal peace that we do not understand. As Mary looks at Him, she can't see the form and the shape. She just sees somebody.

Then He calls her by name.

As a kid outside playing, I could hear my mom calling ten blocks away. I knew that voice. I didn't get her voice mixed up with anybody else's mom.

When Jesus said, "Mary," it rocked her to her soul. She turned. She fell down. She said, "Oh, my teacher!" And she wanted to grab Him. She wanted to react in the familiar way of their relationship.

Jesus said, "No, you can't touch me; I'm still in process. It's this mystery of Me becoming what I'm going to be, and you can't touch Me."

So many times in my faith, I want to make it simple. I want to go to the Bible and read the stories of Jesus and close it there. I want to feel better. I want to find the answer. I want to move on.

But God will not let me stay there. God is calling my name. I think about the stories, the great stories in the Bible. That always seems to be what's happening: God is calling somebody. He's calling them by name. He called Peter. He called Mary. He called Paul by name.

When He does call, there's a part of us that knows it's the resurrected Jesus. It's not just words on a page or stories we want to read for comfort.

There is no dead body. This is mystery. It's incredible. It's unbelievable. But it is really why we are here.

Today, we remember that Jesus is not dead, that Jesus is still calling us by name. Jesus still is trying to lead our lives. Jesus is still about the work of saving this world.

Our job is not to play out a story of our love for Jesus. Our job is to let Jesus love us to God in the mystery of His presence, a presence we do not understand.

When I think about the high moments of my faith, it's the time when that resurrected Jesus comes to me and says, "Steve, Steve." I'm reawakened to that thing I can't understand. And I think, *Is that really Him? Am I making this up myself? Is this crazy?* In my heart, I know I recognize that voice. It reminds me of who I am and what I'm called to do.

So where's Jesus? Did somebody steal Him? Has the world squashed Him? Is there so much evil that He just left us?

No. He's here.

I hear people saying all the time, "I think Jesus has left the building. It's gotten so bad now, we're just waiting for Him to come back."

The truth is that a resurrected Christ has never left us. The work of the kingdom is a God who is moving among us, calling us by name. He moves in and out of our lives and helps us discover what it really means to be alive.

One of my favorite passages of scripture comes from the life of a man who was affected by this resurrected Jesus. Saul was persecuting Christians. He was an outright adversary. Yet it was the resurrected Jesus that came to Saul, renamed him as Paul, and called Paul to a new ministry.

Later in his life, most people think Paul wrote the book of Romans as a reflection on what had happened in his life. Eugene Peterson records those words from Romans 8 like this:

> This resurrection life you received from God is not a timid, grave-tending life. It's adventurously expectant, greeting God with a childlike What's next, Papa? God's Spirit touches our spirits and confirms who we really are. We know who He is, and we know who we are: Father and children. And we know we are going to get what's coming to us—an unbelievable inheritance! We go through exactly what Christ goes through. If we go through the hard times with Him, then we're certainly going to go through the good times with Him!

> None of this fazes us because Jesus loves us. I'm absolutely convinced that nothing—nothing living or dead, angelic or demonic, today or tomorrow, high or low, thinkable or unthinkable—absolutely nothing can get between us and God's love because of the way that Jesus our Master has embraced us.

> You know, this incredible mosaic that's here is a beautiful illustration of the complexity and the very nature of God, the Holy Spirit, the Jesus in person, the presence of the angels, the powers and the principalities.

My friend, the resurrection is not a story about a body that is locked in an empty tomb with a body that somebody stole. But rather, it's a story of a God who has transcended death and walks back and forth between the realms of the eternal and the realms of the temporal calling us by name to a life that is forever.

That's no small stuff. That's no little story. It has no logic, but it does have power.

And so today, I have a question for you. Have you been looking for Jesus in all the wrong places? He's not there. He's right there with you, and He's whispered your name whether you heard it or not. He continues to whisper your name.

He is a close as your breath whether you feel it or not. He is holding you just as if He were embracing a child.

My prayer for you on this Easter Sunday is that you will be still long enough to hear Him.

> Dear God, first we look for salvation in the wrong places. Then we look for Jesus in the wrong places.
>
> The truth is, we don't have to look for Him; He looks for us. The Good Shepherd leaves the ninety-nine sheep and goes after the lost one. He seeks after that little one till He has him.
>
> Dear God, on this Easter Sunday, let us live into the proclamation that Jesus is calling us by name. He knows us. He loves us. And there is nothing that can separate us from Him. Nobody can steal Him. Nobody can take Him. He will not leave us or forsake us because He loves us.
>
> You sent Your Son into the world not to condemn the world, but that the world, through, through Christ, might be saved.
>
> Thank you, Father. Amen.

AFTER EASTER

As we leave the season of Easter, let's talk a little bit about reencountering Jesus when we walk away.

In our household, Easter is an incredible holiday. We probably celebrate it as much or maybe a little more than Christmas. Ever since our daughter Cari was a little girl, she has said, "Daddy, since you preach and Christmases are always tied up, we want everybody to come to our house on Easter."

So we created a tradition where all of Cindy's family comes to our house from all over. They come and worship with us. When I'm not serving a congregation, we have church on the patio. It is always a wonderful time. But then the house kind of empties out as everyone leaves, and we're left with that sense of *Well, that's over with, now what?*

What I found in my own life is that I kind of go through phases like that in my faith. I have those moments when I'm vital and energetic knowing Christ is alive; I've seen the holes in his hands. Then I just have those moments where I feel like Jesus has left the building.

Truthfully, it's not Jesus that's left. Usually it's me. I'm slowly going away. I'm intentionally walking away because I'm either uncomfortable with what Jesus has been doing with me or I've neglected my relationship with Jesus.

Let's look at the story of Peter on the seashore as he had given up. Even after he had seen the resurrected Christ, Peter had returned to fishing. Peter was somebody who had to have Jesus come find him again, and again, and again.

The 20th chapter of John has a passage where Jesus appeared to Mary and then the disciples and Thomas.

> Now Jesus did many other signs in the presence of His disciples which are not written in this book; but these are written so that you may believe that Jesus is the Messiah, the Son of God, and that through believing you may have life in His name.

Whenever Jesus reappears to those on the Emmaus road and finally to Peter on the seashore, I'm reminded of my own faith walk in a very particular way.

The summer that I got the call to ministry was my senior summer. I had finished high school. I had been youth director in my church. And I was left at the end of the summer to preach an evening worship.

I preached the worship service and felt the Holy Spirit alive in my life. As I was closing down the sanctuary, I felt I heard God's voice.

I went down to the altar at Wesley United Methodist Church in Columbus, Mississippi. I knelt down and felt as if Christ put his hands on my shoulders and said, "Steve, I want you to preach."

I was so overwhelmed and humbled. I went and talked to the pastor, Reverend Bill Price. Bill counseled me and guided me. He sent me home to my folks.

After telling everyone, nobody seemed really surprised. And for a little while, I rode on the fumes of that energy. Then something happened.

I had scheduled to enroll at Mississippi State. I was in the cooperative education program where I was working to become an electrical engineer. Somewhere in the midst of the business of prepping for college, I just kind of set that call aside. It was as if it weren't that real anymore. It was as if the practicality of everyday life took over. It's great to be called by Jesus, *but who's going to pay the bills.* I wanted to be an engineer. I've had to go to school. I decided to go and just set that call aside for the time being.

For almost a full semester, I found myself at Mississippi State. Sometimes I went to class, sometimes not. Sometimes I went to Wesley Foundation, sometimes not. At the end of that semester, I finished with a sparkling 2.0 grade point average in engineering; at which time my dad informed me that the funding of my education from his wallet had ended.

What is it that makes us walk away from something as clear as an appearance of Jesus in our lives? How can we be so inconsistent?

Look at Peter. Peter is one of my heroes in the Bible, and I think about how passionate he was. I think in that way, we're a lot alike. I think about how he was energetic and how much he wanted to please Jesus. Sometimes he just went literally overboard.

But then I think about that same Peter that, when he was asked about his faith in Jesus before the crucifixion, denied Him ran away.

That same Peter came back to the room and the gathering of the disciples. When Jesus appeared in that room, he was there.

But, after the crucifixion, Peter went back to his boat. He went back to what he knew, to what was *pre-Jesus.* He went fishing.

What made him do it, do you think?

151

I'll tell you what I think. I think maybe what happened to him is the same thing that happened to me. You know, the call to ministry is a pretty scary thing. When you're just a person, you begin to look at your life and think *What was God thinking? I'm not that good. I have so much work. I don't know if I can spend my whole life doing nothing but what God wants me to do. And there's so much to do. I'm a good man. But I don't understand this. So what if I just go back to normal life and pretend this other didn't happen?*

It's really a reflex of fear. We have an unwillingness to embrace the fact that God knows us better than we do. Jesus knows our giftedness. Jesus knows where we would find happiness, Jesus knows where our life would be most beautifully used in His kingdom.

Yet, somehow, no matter how clear God makes that, we often walk away. We go back to our own designs, our own ways, our own thoughts. And most of it is out of a crisis of confidence.

I want you to marinate in that a minute. I want you to think about your own life, of times when Jesus was really real to you. Then think of times when you felt like you just kind of packed up and headed home.

As we end this journey with the great truth of the resurrection, we talk about Jesus coming back. We talk about Him coming back to Peter. It's a story that I've probably told more than any other story in my ministry.

It's the story of Jesus cooking fish on the seashore, waiting on Peter. Fishing with the others, Peter saw who Jesus was. Peter jumped out of the boat and swam to the shore.

Jesus looked into his eyes and said, "Peter, do you love Me? Do you love Me? Remember, feed my sheep. It's what I called you to do." That moment becomes the seminal moment in Peter's ministry. From there, Peter leaves the boat and becomes the cornerstone of the early Christian church. He does become that rock on which Jesus built His church. Peter steps boldly out on the porch at Pentecost and preaches with passion and thousands of people are led.

What I want us to walk away from this Easter season thinking is this: *Why would we squander the wonder God has nestled for us in our call, to walk away and do what we want to do?*

I'm a firm believer that everyone reading this is called by God. The resurrected Jesus Christ has a word to you, has a place for you, has a mission for you, has a ministry for you. He's waiting for you to hear it, but more than that, to live into it.

Maybe you've heard from God, and you've gone back fishing. You used to go to church, but you now play golf. You used to be involved heavily with youth, but you got disillusioned because they're "just a bunch of sinners up in that church" and you get "sick and tired of the politics."

Well hear these words very clearly from me. Those people do not call you. God does. And you do not follow them, you follow Jesus. He will never disappoint you. And guess what? If you've walked away, you're one of those "sinners" at the church. Truth is, we all are sinners who've either taken life or broken love, squandered life or lost love. And that's not what God intends for us.

Thank you for joining me on this Easter path. I hope, as you think about Easter, you'll ask yourself, *Have I walked away, and is it time for me to go home?*

Let's pray:

Dear God, thank You for Your grace, the fact that nothing will separate us from You and Your love. Even when we walk away, You do not give up.

Thank You for coming down to earth. Thank You for being real. Keep us on the path with You.

Give us the wisdom to turn, to turn, to turn to You. Give us the ears to hear Your words, "Do you love Me?" and to respond, like Peter, to say, "Yes, Lord, we love You."

Let's go, in Jesus' name, Amen.

And always remember to *live loved!*

ABOUT THE AUTHOR

Reverend Steve Casteel is the pastor of First United Methodist Church, Clinton, MS. He served as the Director of Communication and Connectional Ministries for the Mississippi Annual Conference of the United Methodist Church for 7 years. Steve teaches Pastoral Care for Spiritual Formation in the Ms Annual Conference Course of Study and is the Executive Director and Host of *The United Methodist Hour* television ministry.

He received his AA Degree from Wood College, his BA in Social Work from Mississippi State University, and his Masters of Divinity Degree from Emory University. He also participated in the Board of Discipleship's Academy of Preaching and Duke University's United Methodism and American Cultural Study.

Steve is an ordained elder of the Mississippi Conference of the United Methodist Church. He has served as pastor of the Flower Ridge Charge (Louisville, MS), the Pleasant Hill Charge (Olive Branch, MS), Morton United Methodist Church (Morton, MS), Petal United Methodist Church (Petal, MS), St. Matthew's United Methodist Church (Madison, MS), and Forrest Hill UMC (Jackson, MS).

Steve has served on the board of directors of several organizations including American Cancer Society Mid-south Board, Hinton Rural Life Center, The Center for Ministry at Milsaps College, The Milsaps College Board, and the Bethlehem Community Center. He also serves on the Advisory Board for the Mississippi Stop Hunger Now sharehouse in Jackson, MS. He was president of the Mississippi Religious Leadership Conference.

Steve is married to Cindy and they have two wonderful children, Cari and Matt. Cindy is an amazing second grade teacher. Cari is a Doctoral student at Auburn University. Matt is program coordination for Stop Hunger Now.

Steve's guiding mission is to *live loved*.

Made in the USA
Lexington, KY
05 February 2016